JOHNS HOPKINS UNIVERSITY STUDIES
IN
HISTORICAL AND POLITICAL SCIENCE

SERIES XLI

No. 2

THE SHOP COMMITTEE IN THE UNITED STATES

AMS PRESS
NEW YORK

SERIES XLI No. 2

JOHNS HOPKINS UNIVERSITY STUDIES

IN

HISTORICAL AND POLITICAL SCIENCE

Under the Direction of the

Departments of History, Political Economy, and
Political Science

———————

THE SHOP COMMITTEE IN THE UNITED STATES

BY

CARROLL E. FRENCH, Ph.D.

———————

BALTIMORE
THE JOHNS HOPKINS PRESS
1923

Library of Congress Cataloging in Publication Data

French, Carroll Eiker, 1895–
  The shop committee in the United States.

  Reprint. Originally published: Baltimore: Johns
Hopkins Press, 1923. (The Johns Hopkins University
studies in historical and political science; ser. 41,
no. 2)
  Includes bibliographical references and index.
  1. Works councils—United States. I. Title.
II. Series: Johns Hopkins University studies in histori-
cal and political science; ser. 41, no. 2.
HD5660.U5F73   1982   331'.01'12   78-64110
ISBN 0-404-61225-3

AMS PRESS, INC.
56 East 13 Street, New York, N.Y. 10003

This reprint has been authorized by the Johns Hopkins
University Press. Copyright Johns Hopkins University
Press.

Reprinted from the edition of 1923, Baltimore. Trim size
has been slightly altered. Original trim: 15.2 × 24.5 cm.

MANUFACTURED
IN THE UNITED STATES OF AMERICA

CONTENTS

PREFACE

—

This monograph is the result of an investigation carried on while the author was a member of the Economic Seminary of The Johns Hopkins University. It originated from an interest in the introduction of the shop committee in several large corporations and from a desire to discover the relation of this new movement to trade unionism and its possible influence in the field of industrial relations. The chief sources of information have of necessity been documentary. They have comprised mainly the publications of trade unions and of employers' associations, government bulletins and reports, reports of state industrial commissions, and technical and scientific journals. This has been supplemented by personal interviews with managers of industrial relations and by correspondence with from thirty to forty industrial establishments.

The author wishes to express his indebtedness to Professor J. H. Hollander and to Professor G. E. Barnett, who guided the main lines of the investigation and supplied many helpful criticisms and suggestions.

C. E. F.

THE SHOP COMMITTEE IN THE UNITED STATES

INTRODUCTION

The development of collective bargaining has been the outstanding feature of the history of industrial relations. It had its rise with the organization of workmen by trades and crafts and historically the term "Collective Bargaining" has been used exclusively to describe the system of negotiations between trade unions and employers over the question of wages, hours, and working conditions. As expounded by the Webbs and as practiced by the modern trade union, it involves strong organization on the part of both employer and employee, the representation of the workers by their trade union officials, the subordination of the local union to the national organization and the negotiation of standardized wage scales and working rules for the whole industry or trade. This right of the employee to bargain collectively with his employer, in contrast to the individual contract, has won a general and merited recognition.

Until recently, the modern employer has followed one of two courses, collective bargaining with the union, or individual dealings with his employees. But the advent of the shop committee has opened a third course. The shop committee, as introduced and developed in the United States, is based upon the idea of bargaining between the employees and employer of individual plants or the plants of one employer. It rests on the assumption that the normal economic relationship of labor and capital is in the individual factory; that industrial government should function within the productive units rather than between national organizations of these

9

units. It has grown up outside of trade unionism and has flourished especially in unorganized industries.

The shop committee may be defined as a form of organization for collective dealing by means of joint committees, composed of an equal number of representatives of both employees and employer, chosen from within a single plant or corporation. In form it varies from the single shop committee of the small concern to the elaborate committee systems of large corporations based upon representation by departments and plants. One writer has defined the shop committee as "a system of government composed of a series of committees, with duties which differ but slightly, and which is organized and operated upon the principle, that as far as is practical, the relations between employer and employee should be adjusted by common counsel at joint meetings of accredited representatives of each side."[1]

In popular articles such systems have been given a variety of names: Shop Councils, Plant Plans of Representation or Collective Bargaining, Employee Representation, and Industrial Democracy. Although known by these various names, the shop committee, as such, is marked by certain very definite characteristics. These are:

(1) The division of a plant into voting units on some selected basis, generally by crafts, departments, or shops.

(2) The election of representatives by the employees, in mass meetings of their own or by secret ballot.

(3) A system of joint committees formed on the principle of equal representation of both men and management.

(4) Discussion and adjustment of all matters of mutual concern by negotiations between such committees and representatives of the management.

Some provision for an appeal by either party to an impartial board or neutral tribunal, while not an essential feature of the shop committee, is usually found in the majority of plans. The distinctive feature of the shop committee is that as a system of collective dealing centered in the single plant,

---

[1] Stoddard, The Shop Committee, p. 27.

it constitutes a permanent machinery for contact between the management and the men. It introduces into the plant the institution of collective dealing as a continuing and normal process of the industry.

The term shop committee, however, must not be taken to mean all forms of workmen's committees found in shops. There have been committees of various kinds composed of employees in shops from the very beginning of unions. Some of them have been part of the trade union organization, like the printer's Chapel or the local Pit Committee in the mine workers' organization. Many employee committees exist which function with respect to safety or to some aspect of welfare work. In many firms there are committees of employees who act in an advisory capacity and with whom the management consults at its pleasure. These isolated committees must not be confused with the shop committee. The shop committee, as a system of collective dealing, does not exist until it involves the representation of all the workmen of a plant, upon joint committees, which negotiate, on an equal basis with the management, questions of wages, hours, and working and living conditions.

Neither is the shop committee to be represented as synonymous with industrial democracy. The majority of plans in operation have involved little or no sacrifice in control on the part of the management. The most that can be said for the shop committee is that both parties are pledged to accept the decisions of their joint committee. Even then, the final decision rests with the management, although, in the experience of the shop committee, the persistent rejection of the findings of the joint committees is considered a breach of faith. There is usually a provision for an appeal to impartial arbitration.

It is necessary at this point to make clear the exact position of the shop committee with reference to trade union collective bargaining. Much confusion has resulted from the indiscriminate use of the term collective bargaining. In the First Industrial Conference called by the President, October 1919, the employers' group openly professed allegiance to the principle of collective bargaining and in the same breath declared themselves in favor of shop committees, which in their opinion fully satisfied the conditions.   This stand was not only inconsistent but the application of the term collective bargaining to shop committees was misleading, and, to the extent that it was deliberate, was highly disingenuous.   The shop committee, contrary to the popular idea, does not imply collective bargaining.

The truth is that the trade union and the shop committees are diametrically opposed in principle.[2]   They represent two distinct and conflicting systems of industrial relations.   Collective bargaining implies national agreements arrived at through conferences between national trade unions and national associations of employers.   Underlying it is the right of the employee to be represented by representatives of his own choosing, from whatever source derived.   The shop committee, on the other hand, means collective dealing within the local plant, negotiation by means of permanent joint committees made up of an equal number of representatives of the men and the management.   The right of the employee to be represented by representatives of his own choosing is restricted by the necessity of choosing his representatives from among his own number, bona fide employees of the plant or firm concerned.   The term collective bargaining has always been used to embrace the trade union idea of bargaining.   It is a misnomer to use it in connection with the shop committee which in its fundamental principles presents such a contrast to trade unionism.

---

[2] Three fundamental differences between the trade union and the shop committee have been pointed out by Paul H. Douglas in an article on " Shop Committees: Substitutes for, or Supplement to, Trade Unions? " in Journal of Political Economy, Feb. 1921, p. 91, as follows:

" 1. The shop committee represents the workmen of only one plant or company while the union represents the workmen of many plants in a given trade or industry.

2. The management is not excluded from the meetings of the shop committee, whereas it is from the meetings of the union.

3. The shop committees in the U. S. . . . are initiated by employers, while the unions are initiated by the workers."

Some writers have urged that there is no inherent conflict between the shop committee and the trade union and that the two plans are found in some industries operating harmoniously side by side.[3]   Such a case can be made out only by a juggling of terms.   For one thing, the shop committee presumes no recognition of the right of trade union officials to represent the workers.   The trade union could not allow local autonomy in the negotiation of the wage scale.   A combination of the two would result in neither the present shop committee nor the present trade union.   There cannot exist at the same time collective dealings through the shop committee and an honest recognition of the trade union.   The two are incompatible in theory and mutually exclusive in practice.

There are in reality two labor movements in the United States at the present time, one the regular trade union movement and the other the shop committee movement.   In order to avoid confusion in terminology, it has been thought best to retain the use of the term " collective bargaining " in its proper sense, as descriptive of the trade union system.   To designate the system represented by the shop committee, the term " collective dealing " will be used throughout the investigation.

Although the shop committee is having a rapid development in Germany, France, England and other European countries, the scope of this investigation has been limited to the United States.   The shop committee cannot be studied without reference to the labor movements surrounding it and the problems raised in one country are fully ample for a single research. The purpose of this investigation is in general: first, to discover and set forth the principles of the shop committee and the form it has taken in this country; second, to discover the strength and weakness of the shop committee as revealed by an analysis of its operation; third, to work out the relation of the shop committee to the trade union; and in the last place,

---

[3] " The Shop committee representation plan does not in any way whatsoever conflict with organized labor; in fact in many instances shop committees have been formed with the approval of the local organized labor body " (Outlook, June 1920).

to arrive at some conclusions as to the permanent contributions of the shop committee and its influence on the future development of industrial relations.

In the first chapter an attempt will be made to trace the history of the shop committee in the United States. No attempt at description or critical analysis will be made. The aim will be to set forth as clearly as possible the progress of the movement from its introduction up to the present time and its relation to the accompanying events in the history of industrial relations of the last ten years. Special emphasis will be given to the shop committee during the period of the Government War Labor Agencies, for it was during this period that the shop committee began to exert a real influence on industrial relations.

The second chapter will be devoted to a description of the various plans and forms of shop committees now in operation. While there is a different plan for almost every shop, there are certain outstanding plans which best illustrate the form which the shop committee has taken in this country.

The third chapter will be a critical analysis of the working of these plans in detail. The success of the shop committee is largely dependent upon its operation. It has been tried long enough for a fair estimate to be given of its accomplishments. The claims of its advocates and the accusations of its opponents will be tested by the results achieved.

The fourth chapter will deal with the problem of the trade union and the shop committee. An effort will be made to discover the position of trade union leaders on the shop committee and to outline their policy. The strength of their arguments will be examined and the grounds for their attitude criticized. Conclusions will be presented as to the future relation of the two movements. The chapter will close with an estimate of the future influence of the shop committee as a system of collective dealing on the development of industrial relations.

CHAPTER I

The History of the Shop Committee in the United States

The Pre-War Period.—The credit for the pioneer installation of a shop committee in the United States is claimed by Mr. H. F. J. Porter, Vice President and General Manager of the Nernst Lamp Company, Pittsburgh, Pa.[1] This company was then a small organization, employing only about one hundred and fifty men and women and engaged in the manufacture of electrical supplies. In the winter of 1903–1904, Mr. Porter, being convinced of the necessity of arousing greater interest among his employees and desiring a closer cooperation between the men and the management, called a meeting of his force and requested them to elect a permanent " factory committee." This committee was composed of representatives from the clerical force, from the shop operatives and from the foremen. The Company was represented by the superintendent, who acted as permanent chairman of the committee. There was no attempt here to set up an industrial government of any kind, no administrative authority was granted to the committee. It was merely an organ through which the employees might make known their wants to the management and through which the management might get into closer touch with the men. The management had always desired from time to time to confer with the men but there had been no established machinery. Mr. Porter, referring to the newly established committee, said: " Here . . . was as representative a committee as could be obtained ready at all times to consider such matters and to pass upon them intelligently for recommendation to the management, and a channel

---

[1] H. F. J. Porter, " Origin and Purpose of the Shop Committee," in bulletin of the New Jersey State Chamber of Commerce, vol. vi, No. 10.

of intercommunication between management and employees existed continuously." [2]

There is record of an " advisory committee plan " instituted in the American Rolling Mill Company in 1904.[3]   In 1905, Mr. E. A. Filene set up a system of shop committees among the employees of his department store in Boston, and in 1907, a plan of employee representation was installed by the Nelson Valve Company, of Philadelphia, a small factory employing about one hundred men.[4]   It provided for a lower house or " works committee " composed of representatives elected by the men, one from each department, and presided over by a chairman elected from their own number. A second committee or advisory board was organized, composed of foremen and presided over by the superintendent. These two committees met in joint session once a month, for the purpose of discussing grievances, conferring over suggestions and attending to other matters of mutual interest.[5]

In 1912 appeared the first adoption of a shop committee commonly known as " the United States Government " type. It was introduced by Mr. John Leitch, an apostle of " Industrial Democracy," a term which he defined as " The organization of any factory or business institution into a little democratic state with a representative government which shall have both its legislative and executive phases." [6]   The plan provided for the organization of the personnel of a company into a house of representatives for the employees, a senate composed of foremen and minor executives, and a cabinet comprising the executive officials. Each body had powers and methods of procedure similar to those of the Federal Government.

The introduction of this plan by the Packard Piano Company led to its adoption by other firms and gave rise to a lively discussion of employee representation. For the first

[2] Engineering Magazine, Aug. 1905, pp. 645-647.
[3] Iron Age, Nov. 10, 1921, p. 1207.
[4] Porter, Origin and Purpose of the Shop Committee.
[5] Outlook, Mar. 13, 1909.
[6] John Leitch, Man to Man, The Story of Industrial Democracy, p. 140.

time, the shop committee came into contact with the local trade union. In one plant the shop committee followed an unsuccessful strike for recognition of the union, in another it was the means of forestalling an attempted organization of the factory; [7] in several plants the existence of the shop committee was menaced by the unions and the friction resulted in strikes. The success of these more or less primitive committee systems was, however, sufficient to give the movement momentum. By 1919 this type of shop committee had been adopted by about twenty American firms, including the William Demuth Company of New York, Sydney Blumenthal & Company, Shelton, Conn., the Atlantic Refining Company, and the American Multigraph Company, both of Cleveland, Ohio. The Leitch Plan has not, however, been extended. It has been limited to comparatively small firms where the problem of representation was relatively simple. It is not a representative type of the American shop committee and has given way to more modern forms.

In 1915, the shop committee as a plan for employee representation was introduced for the first time into a large corporation. Following a bitter but fruitless strike for the recognition of the union, which resulted in a personal visit by Mr. John D. Rockefeller, Jr., a plan of industrial representation was offered to the employees of the Colorado Fuel and Iron Company. It went into effect October 2, 1915. A report of the Colorado Coal Commission dwelt at great length on the new plan of employee representation.[8] It said in part:

> The plan of the Colorado Fuel and Iron Co. to regulate by contract its relation with its own employees and to provide under the terms of the said contract for the adjustment of grievances is also a new departure in the United States. Indeed, your Commission knows of nothing just like it in force anywhere. The importance of it, as an effort on the part of a large corporation to regulate its relations with its own employees by contracting with them, instead of through a trade agreement made with a labor union, justifies your Commission in discussing this plan with great care.

[7] Ibid., pp. 31, 191–192.
[8] Portion of the report, reprinted in Industry and Humanity, by King, pp. 442–443.

2

The inauguration of this plan of employee representation by a corporation of the size and standing of the Colorado Fuel and Iron Company gave rise to a wide discussion of the shop committee. The Company employed about twelve thousand men, divided almost equally between the coal mines and a large steel mill. The twenty or more mining camps were scattered over the State of Colorado, largely in districts devoid of any municipal organization. Only twenty-one per cent of the employees were native Americans. The plan was openly a substitute for trade union collective bargaining. Unbiased critics, however, gave Mr. Rockefeller credit for more than a mere desire to avoid trade union recognition.[9] For a corporation whose traditional labor policy had so long ignored the slightest claims of labor to representation and had insisted upon individual bargaining, the change to a policy of collective dealing through joint committees of its own men was a big step forward. The constitution and technique of the Colorado plan was closely studied, and definitely influenced the forms of shop committees which followed.

The adoption of the Colorado Plan ended the first distinct period in the history of the shop committee. Its introduction seems to have been inspired by a desire to establish a closer relation between management and men and to stimulate the interests of employees in production. The committees were elementary in structure and in most cases purely advisory in function. The Leitch Plan was the most elaborate but had no joint committee. All the plans were initiated by employers. While it is difficult to analyze motives, the facts are that all of the plans originated in open shops or followed upon the failure of the union to establish itself. As yet, however, there appears to be no effort to substitute the shop committee for an existing practice of collective bargaining. The two movements, as movements, can hardly be said to have come into conflict with each other.

The War Period.—With the regulation of war labor by the

---

[9] Report of Colorado Coal Commission, quoted by King in Industry and Humanity, p. 443.

Federal Government, the shop committee entered upon the second period of its development. The Shipbuilding Labor Adjustment Board, acting as a central board of arbitration for the shipbuilding industry, found that too many cases were coming before it and that their proper adjustment called for an unusual amount of technical and local knowledge. The shop committee was therefore introduced as a form of local machinery to handle grievances on the spot, speedily and effectively, and as a medium through which the technical skill and knowledge of local conditions could be used in their adjustment.[10]

In October 1917, an award of the Board ordered the formation of shop committees among the shipyards of the Portland District.[11] By a decision, March 4, 1918, they were extended to the South Atlantic and Gulf yards and soon after to the yards of the North Atlantic and the Great Lakes Districts.[12] On October 24, 1918, the Board authorized the use of shop committees for all shipyards where the owners were "not parties to joint agreements with the labor organizations of their respective districts."[13] Owing to the opposition of the unions, the committees authorized were not set up in the Delaware District nor in the yards adjacent to Seattle and San Francisco.

The committees installed under the supervision of the Shipbuilding Labor Adjustment Board at first functioned poorly and were in general a practical failure. The reasons given for this were, (1) lack of proper organization of the committees, (2) the indifference of the workers consequent upon the high wages, and (3) the open jealousy and hostility of the trade unions. In one district the committees were completely ignored; over eighty per cent of the grievances were taken up by the business agents of the unions directly with the

---

[10] Douglas and Wolfe, "Labor Administration in the Shipbuilding Industry during War Time," in Journal of Political Economy, vol. xxvii, p. 370.
[11] Ibid.
[12] Text of Award, Monthly Labor Review, May 1918, p. 138.
[13] Douglas and Wolfe, p. 370; Text of Award, Monthly Labor Review, June 1918, p. 201.

Board's Examiner. By December 1918, however, these conditions had been remedied and a majority of the shop committees were functioning with a fair degree of success. There was a reduction in the number of grievances coming before the central arbitration board, and a speedy settlement of many minor disputes on the ground cut off potential strikes, making possible uninterrupted production.

The shop committee also found a place in the arbitration machinery of the United States Railroad Administration.[14] Commenting on the labor policy of the Railroad Administration, one writer said: "The most important contribution of the Railroad Administration's labor adjustment system has been its successful promotion of the local shop committee."[15] The General Board of Railway Wages and Working Conditions was created by the Director General, March 22, 1918. It was composed of three railroad officials and three trade union officials. Under this board were four Departmental Boards of Adjustment, likewise composed of a joint membership. Before resort could be had to these Boards, or an appeal taken to the Director of the Division of Labor, the grievances had to be first brought before local shop committees, created by order of the Director General. Only after failure to settle the grievance in the local committee was it possible to appeal the case to the regular tribunals. As a result, it is reported that the vast majority of grievances never reached the General Board and that local railroad labor became accustomed to settle their grievances through local negotiations.

In May 1918, the United States Fuel Administration was party to an agreement between the miners and operators of the Maryland and Upper Potomac region which provided, among other things, for the creation of mine or shop committees to handle grievances. The settlement provided specifically: "Mine committees shall be elected and the manage-

---

[14] A. M. Bing, "Work of the Wage Adjustment Boards," in Journal of Political Economy, June 1919, vol. xxvii, p. 436.
[15] Wehle, "War Labor Policies and Their Outcome in Peace," in Quarterly Journal of Economics, vol. xxxiii, p. 334.

ment shall receive such committees, to adjust disputes which
the superintendent and the mine foreman, and the employee
or employees affected are unable to adjust." As the result
of a conference between the Federal Fuel Administrator and
the International Officials of the United Mine Workers of
America,[16] this scheme was accepted by all parties for the
whole industry. It was further provided that in case it was
impossible to reach a settlement, the dispute was to be referred to an Umpire appointed by the United States Fuel
Administrator.

In its use by the Shipbuilding Labor Adjustment Board,
the United States Railroad Administration and the Fuel Administration, the shop committee functioned purely as a device to settle grievances. Little attention was paid to working out the detail of the organization of the committees, and
in many cases they were never set up. In some instances
they met with violent opposition from the unions; in others
they were introduced by joint agreement with the unions.
They served to demonstrate the advantages of some form of
local, permanent machinery for maintaining relations between
workmen and their employees, and to bring the shop committee into wider notice.

In the hands of the National War Labor Board the shop
committee took a dominant and important part. It was introduced not merely as an instrument for the local adjustment of grievances, but as a fully developed plan of collective
dealing for the employees of the entire plant.

One of the first discoveries of the Government in its war
experience was that the absence of means for collective bargaining was largely responsible for industrial unrest and disturbances. Early in the fall of 1917 severe strikes in several
fields interfered with production vitally important for war
needs. The President appointed a Mediation Commission to
investigate labor disturbances and to effect a settlement in the
Arizona copper fields, the California oil fields, and the packing industry. On January 9, 1918, the Commission sub-

---

[16] Monthly Labor Review, Sept. 1918, p. 186.

mitted its report.[17]   With reference to the Arizona copper
fields it declared that the dominant feeling of protest was
"that the Industry was conducted upon an autocratic basis.
The workers did not have representation in determining those
conditions of their employment which vitally affected their
lives as well as the company's output."   What the men
wanted was "the power to secure industrial justice in matters
of vital concern to them."   In a summary of its investigations, the Commission laid down two fundamental causes for
the prevailing industrial unrest:

(1) Broadly speaking, American industry lacks a healthy basis of
relationship between management and men.   At bottom this is due to
the insistence by employers upon individual dealings with their men.
Direct dealings with employee's organizations is still the minority
rule in the United States.   In the majority of instances there is no
joint dealing and in too many instances employers are in active opposition to labor organizations.
(2) Widespread lack of knowledge on the part of capital as to
labor's feelings and needs and on the part of labor as to the problems of management.   This is due primarily to a lack of collective
negotiations as a normal processs of industry.

In its actual work the Commission in each case made a
War-Time Agreement covering the industry, which included,
in addition to the provision for an orderly adjustment of all
disputes, the establishment of permanent channels of com-
munication between management and men through grievance
committees.   The settlement of the dispute in the packing industry by the Commission provided for the principle of collective dealing through representatives elected by the employees.   The Commission followed its declared principle
that "working conditions of industry should normally be determined by the parties themselves."

Following the report of the President's Mediation Commission, came the formation of the War Labor Conference
Board in January 1918.   It was composed of an equal number of representatives from both labor and capital and in its
report submitted to the Secretary of Labor, March 29, 1918,
it recommended the formation of the National War Labor

---

[17] Ibid., Feb. 1918.

Board, as an agency for arbitration and adjustment of all disputes in war industries. The Board was founded by Presidential proclamation, April 6, 1918, and among the principles laid down for the guidance of the Board were the following: [18]

(1) The right of workers to organize in trade unions and to bargain collectively through chosen representatives is recognized and affirmed.

(2) The right of employers to organize in associations or groups and to bargain collectively through chosen representatives is recognized and affirmed.

(3) Employers should not discharge workers for membership in trade unions nor for legitimate trade-union activities.

(4) The workers in their exercise of their right to organize shall not use coercive measures of any kind to induce employers to bargain or to deal therewith, nor to induce persons to join their organization.

(a) In establishments where union shop exists, the same shall continue and the union standards as to wages, hours of labor, and other conditions of employment shall be maintained.

(b) In establishments where union and non-union men and women now work together and the employer meets only with employees or representatives engaged in said establishments, the continuance of such a condition shall not be deemed a grievance. This declaration is not intended in any manner to deny the right or discourage the practice of the formation of labor unions or the joining of the same by the workers in said establishments, as guaranteed in the last paragraph, nor to prevent the War Labor Board from urging, or any umpire from granting, under the machinery herein provided, improvements in their situation in matters of wages, hours of labor, or other conditions as shall be found desirable from time to time.

In view of these principles and in the light of what experience the Government had already achieved in adjusting war-time labor relations, the immediate adoption of the shop committee by the National War Labor Board was but a natural development. The Shipbuilding Labor Adjustment Board had used the shop committee as a much needed feature of its arbitration machinery. It had demonstrated beyond doubt the need for some permanent local machinery for negotiation between men and management. Moreover, the demands of war-time production resulted in the steady creation of new problems such as overtime, absenteeism, problems of technique, matters requiring local machinery for the most efficient solution.

---

[18] Wehle, Quarterly Journal of Economics, vol. xxxiii, p. 328.

Finally, the endorsement of the principle of collective bargaining created a problem for the Board in those industries where the union was not recognized. The principles laid down for the guidance of the War Labor Board virtually amounted to a declared truce between the unions and employers. The unions promised not to strike or to use coercive measures and in return were guaranteed the right to collective bargaining. At the same time the Government promised not to force the recognition of the union upon the employer. Where the union was already recognized, no trouble would arise. But, in the words of one of the administrators of the Board, in the majority of American industries there was "a sheer lack of machinery designed to eliminate internal shop friction, whether over large matters or small matters." [19] In these industries the Board was under the necessity of providing some substitute for collective bargaining. The shop committee was already at hand to be used in the solution of this problem.

From the very first, the shop committee was promoted at every opportunity by the War Labor Board as a substitute for collective bargaining.[20] Provision for its installation and use is found in more than one hundred and twenty-five of the awards. In the majority of awards the procedure as to installation and elections of committees was left to be worked out by the parties concerned. However, the most important of the shop committee systems introduced under the jurisdiction of the Board were worked out by the Board itself and installed under the supervision of its own examiners.

One of the first plans to be installed by the Board was instituted in the Pittsfield Works of the General Electric Company. Late in June 1918, this Company was ordered to eliminate individual employment contracts and to substitute a plan of plant collective dealing by means of shop committees. The problem of working out the basis of representation, the

---

[19] Stoddard, The Shop Committee, p. 9.
[20] "War Labor Policies and Their Outcome in Peace," in Quarterly Journal of Economics, Feb. 1919, p. 321.

election procedure, qualification of workers to act as representatives and other details of the plan were stipulated by the award or adjusted by the Examiner appointed by the Board to install the system.

The Pittsfield plan was one of the first attempts of the War Labor Board to put the principle of the shop committee into practice and it was not satisfied with the result achieved. They felt that it was, as a practical system, incomplete and represented only a beginning. From experience gathered in subsequent installations of shop committees the Board gradually worked out a somewhat standardized type of shop committee, which, while it was not presumed to be adapted to every kind of industry, embodied fundamental principles which experience had proved practical. The type of shop committee finally evolved by the Board was set up in the Lynn Plant of the General Electric Company.

The shop committees instituted by the National War Labor Board were by no means impotent organizations. The importance of the duties laid upon them made them a real factor in the decision of all matters of mutual interest to employees and employer. The functions of the committees were not limited to interpretation of awards. The decisions of the National War Labor Board often consisted solely of an order to set up collective dealing by shop committees, throwing upon the shop committees the actual task of adjusting wages, piece-rates, hours, questions of overtime, classification of workers and even questions of shop discipline. The first task of a joint committee, newly created by an award, was often the framing of a new wage scale for the entire plant. The range of matters coming within the scope of the War Labor Board committees were entirely as broad as that of a trade union working agreement.

The decisions of the Board were characterized by a steady and almost severe insistence that collective dealing be established as a normal process in industry. It considered the installation of collective dealing of more importance than the immediate adjustment of grievances, and in many cases refused to decide the particular matters in dispute until the parties had failed to adjust the matters themselves, through their committees.[21]   The Board forced employers to meet and to deal with committees of their employees regardless of whether they were composed of or elected by union men.[22] Even where the representative chosen by the employees was an agent of the local union, the Board, through its Umpire, held that the workmen were entitled to "meet their employer through and by a representative or representatives of their own choice whether such representative be at the time an employee in the establishment or not."[23]

The majority of committees established by the National War Labor Board were set up during the summer of 1918 and the early months of 1919.   Evidence of the stimulus to the growth of shop committees given by Federal War Labor Agencies is seen in the fact that out of two hundred and twenty-five Works Councils formed since January 1, 1918, one hundred and twenty, or fifty-three per cent, were created by these agencies.   Eighty-six were created by the National War Labor Board, and thirty-one by the Shipbuilding Labor Adjustment Board.[24]

As a result of its use by these agencies the shop committee seemed to have secured a permanent position.   One writer says:

The local shop committee has been planted so well and so broadly throughout industry by these various governmental adjustment agencies as hardly to seem eradicable. Promoted from the outset by the Shipbuilding Labor Adjustment Board, later by the President's Mediation Commission in the Arizona Copper District and in the Packing establishments; firmly established subsequently by the Labor Board in widely divergent fields of industrial activity which had never known its use, and finally made a thoroughly integrated part of a machinery for adjustment extending over the entire American Railroad system, the shop committee has secured a strong position.

---

[21] Cases of the National War Labor Board, Docket No. 416.   The cases of the Board are indicated hereafter by the abbreviation, N. W. L. B. cases.
[22] N. W. L. B. Cases, Employees vs. Pacific Electric Railway Co.
[23] N. W. L. B. Cases, Machinists vs. Niles-Bement Pond Co. of Plainfield, N. J.
[24] Report of the National Industrial Conference Board, p. 13.

Whatever reaction is to be expected toward pre-war industrial relations could hardly sweep away a method so widely employed and in
essence so akin to the germs of American institutions.[25]

But in connection with the view expressed above it must be
remembered that the installation of the shop committee by the
war labor adjustment boards was semi-compulsory; that the
government policy was an emergency policy. The régime of
collective dealing through committees of employees was in
effect a practical reversal of the labor policy of many companies and in the vast majority of cases was virtually forced
upon reluctant employers. In all such cases the shop committees were immediately abandoned with the cessation of
government control of industry. In contrast to the antagonism of employers, the Trade Unions, with some exceptions,
had viewed with favor the introduction of the shop committee
and had cooperated in its use. Yet here also the situation is
to be explained in large measure by the suppression of the
right of trade unions to strengthen their organization during
the war.

The Post-War Period.—The period from the Armistice to
the present time has witnessed three important developments
in the history of the shop committee. First, there has been
an actual increase in the number of shop committees established, and an extension of the movement into new types of
industries; second, the war-time opposition of large numbers
of employers has given way to an open endorsement, especially among those actively allied with the movement for the
open shop; third, by reason of its increasing use as a substitute for union recognition, the shop committee has drawn
upon itself the bitter opposition of the American Trade Union
movement.

The number of shop committees in operation has shown a
steady increase since January 1919. Of those set up by the
war labor boards, it is safe to say that a majority continued
in existence after the abolition of government control. To
these have been added from time to time shop committee
plans sponsored always by employers, many of them heads of

---

[25] Wehle, Quarterly Journal of Economics, vol. xxxiii, p. 336.

large corporations.   The shop committee was introduced into the Inland Steel Company in January 1919.[26]   This was followed by the adoption of Works Councils in nineteen plants of the International Harvester Company.   The Willys-Overland Company announced the adoption of a plan of employee representation on May 2, 1919, and in July the employees of the Goodyear Tire and Rubber Company elected representatives under a shop committee plan.   On May 20, 1921, the Pennsylvania Railroad announced its intention of setting up a system of shop committees.[27]   This was the first application of the principle of collective dealing to a large transportation system.   In August 1921, the shop committee was introduced into the plant of Armour & Company, of Chicago, and in three other of the larger packing establishments.[28]

The increase of shop committees on the railroads has been the most significant development in the recent history of the movement.   The leadership of the Pennsylvania Railroad in this respect has been noted above.   As early as December 21, 1920,[29] at a meeting between the officials of the road and the local divisional chairmen of the employees in the engine and train service, a system of joint committees was approved, leading up to a General Joint Reviewing Committee to handle all cases appealed from the divisional and regional joint committees.   On May 20, 1921, committees were elected by the Shop Crafts and the Maintenance of Way Employees and since then the plan has been extended to the Telegraphers, Signal Department, Marine Department, etc., affecting in all one hundred and fifty thousand employees.[30]   Through these committees set up in the various departments, wage agreements and working schedules were negotiated for the whole Pennsylvania system.

The strike of the railway shopmen in the summer of 1922 was the immediate cause for the rapid extension of shop com-

[26] This plan was later abandoned. Letter, Jan. 23, 1922.
[27] Railway Age, June 1921.
[28] New York Times, Nov. 19, 1921.
[29] "Employee Representation on the Pennsylvania Railroad System," in Bulletin Issued by the Pennsylvania Railroad, p. 6.
[30] Bulletin of the Pennsylvania Railroad.

mittees to a number of important railroads. Among these
were the Delaware and Hudson, the Nashville, Chattanooga
and St. Louis, the Central Railroad of New Jersey, the Le-
high Valley, and the New York, New Haven and Hartford
Railroad. In all, it was reported that sixteen roads with a
total mileage of fifty-five thousand, not including the Pennsylvania System, established shop committees in their mechan-
ical departments and negotiated agreements with them.[31]

There have been various estimates of the number of shop
committees now in existence, but they are at best only fair
approximations. One investigation carried out in August
1919, obtained reports on two hundred and twenty-five shop
committees, organized in one hundred and seventy-six companies or corporations, employing from four hundred thousand to five hundred thousand men.[32] A partial list issued by
the United States Department of Labor contains the names
of one hundred and seventy-eight business organizations with
some form of the shop committee. According to the estimate of Professor Paul Douglas, the shop committee has been
organized in " between three and four hundred business establishments employing between a half a million and a million
workmen.[33] Making a fair allowance for lapse of plans and
for the rate of increase, this last estimate may be taken as
fairly representative of the actual situation.

The shop committee is found in nearly all the important
branches of industry. It has acquired a firm hold in the iron
and steel industries, machine manufacturing, coal and iron
mining, textiles, food products, and public service corporations. It has recently been introduced into a national railway system and into the packing industry. Out of the two
hundred and twenty-five work councils investigated by the
National Industrial Conference Board, one hundred and
forty-four were in the metal trades. It was also found that
" Works Councils are predominantly found in establishments
employing large numbers of workers." [34]

[31] New York Times, October 14, 1922.
[32] Nat. Indus. Conf. Board, Research Report No. 21.
[33] Journal of Political Economy, Feb. 1921, p. 89.
[34] Nat. Indus. Conf. Board, Research Report No. 21, pp. 14, 15.

The progress of the shop committee since the war has also been characterized by a marked increase in its approval by employers. First, the shop committee has recommended itself to employers for whom it has replaced the old system of individual contract by the new plan of collective dealing. It has also come to appeal to those employers who see in it a most welcome substitute for collective bargaining through the trade union. In a statement of principles submitted by the employers' group to the President's First Industrial Conference held in Washington, D. C., October 1919, the employers put themselves squarely in favor of collective dealing through shop committees.[35] They held that the establishment, rather than the whole industry, should be the unit of production; that plans for " collective bargaining " were most desirable which secured and developed contact and full opportunity for exchange of views within the individual plant; they openly urged the use of shop committees as opposed to representation of employees by union officials. The shop committee was later endorsed by the United States Chamber of Commerce [36] and by many other employer associations.[37] In March 1920, the Report of the President's Second Industrial Conference endorsed the shop committee as a desirable form of collective dealing.[38] This stand met the approval of employers everywhere and did much to increase the interest in the development of the movement.

The final development in the history of the shop committee has been the open opposition of the American Trade Union movement. It is the culmination of local clashes between the unions and the shop committees which began during the war and increased in frequency and bitterness from the Armistice on. In the spring of 1919 the shop committee of the Western Union Telegraph Company helped to defeat the union in a

---

[35] Proceedings of the First Industrial Conference, pp. 80–82.
[36] Special Bulletin No. 31, United States Chamber of Commerce, Sept. 1, 1920. Referendum submitted to members by a large majority endorsed open shop collective dealings, represented by the shop committee.
[37] Cleveland Chamber of Commerce, New York Times, Mar. 1, 1920.
[38] Report of the Industrial Conference, Mar. 6, 1920, pp. 6–7, 9–12.

strike for recognition. The efforts to organize the steel industry early came in contact with the shop committee plans of many of the steel companies. In June 1919, the leaders in the attempt to organize the steel industry were successful in getting the Atlantic City Convention of the American Federation of Labor to pass a resolution condemning all shop committee systems and representation plans.[39] This was followed by an attack upon the shop committee plan of the Midvale Steel and Ordnance Company at Johnstown, Pa. The plan of the Colorado Fuel and Iron Company was ineffectual in preventing a strike in September 1919. The plan of representation was bitterly denounced by the union, which declared that ninety-eight per cent of the men had voted to abolish it and were determined to have nothing except trade union collective bargaining.

It was not long before the official heads of the labor movement were forced to declare themselves. The crisis arose at the First Industrial Conference held in Washington from October 6 to 23. Here, Samuel Gompers, President of the American Federation of Labor, came out openly against the shop committee and announced the intention of organized labor to fight it to the end.[40] The stand of the employers for, and the unflinching opposition of the labor group to, collective dealing through shop committees, finally disrupted the Conference. The report of the Second Industrial Conference held in March 1920, was denounced by the Montreal Convention of the A. F. of L. because it had urged the use of shop committees as means of collective bargaining.[41]

The two most recent extensions of the shop committee system have been bitterly opposed by organized labor. The adoption of the shop committee by the Chicago packers was followed shortly by a strike of the Amalgamated Association of Meat Cutters and Butcher Workmen of North America.[42] The efforts of the Pennsylvania Railroad to introduce its sys-

[39] Proceedings of the Atlantic Convention of the A. F. of L.
[40] Proceedings of the First Industrial Conference, pp. 232–233.
[41] Proceedings of the Montreal Convention of the A. F. of L.
[42] New York Times, Nov. 19, 1921.

tem of shop committees have been contested by the Federated Shop Crafts affiliated with the American Federation of Labor and the dispute was carried through the Railway Labor Board into the Federal Courts.   In the litigation which ensued, the Pennsylvania Railroad was upheld in its right to recognize employees duly elected, as representatives of the shopmen, even though not members of the union.   As a result of the shopmen's strike, the Federated Shop Crafts were defeated, the shop committees now being the only medium of representation open to the employees.

The ultimate working out of the conflict between these two systems, collective bargaining and collective dealing, cannot but have a great influence upon the development of industrial relations in the United States.   The shop committee has developed from a stage of individual experimentation to a well-developed system of collective dealing, with a lengthening period of experience behind it and a powerful group of adherents.   It promises to be a permanent factor in whatever system of industrial relations is developed in the United States.

CHAPTER II

Form and Organization of the Shop Committee

Ever since the introduction of the shop committee into the United States, it has exhibited a variety of types. These have resulted from wide differences in the size, character and local conditions of the industries concerned. One report distinguishes five major groups, namely:[1]

(1) The War Labor Board type.

(2) Shop committee systems combined with unionism.

(3) The Rockefeller type.

(4) The Federal type (John Leitch).

(5) Cooperative type with representation on the board of directors.

Another investigation classifies shop committee systems according to the author of the plan, supplemented by the functions assigned to the committees:[2]

(1) Plans set up by the National War Labor Board.

(2) Committees set up by the Shipbuilding Labor Adjustment Board.

(3) Shop committee plans set up by employers.

> (a) "Limited Works" councils.
>
> (b) "Company Union" plans.
>
> (c) "Industrial Democracy" plans.
>
> (d) Other types of employer plans.

It is not the purpose of this investigation to work out a new classification. To evaluate the shop committee, it is more important to show the detailed organization and the fundamental features of the prevailing plans than to set forth a description of all the types that have at some time been tried. Out of a comparatively brief history there has evolved

---

[1] Report of New Jersey Bureau of State Research No. 10, July 1919, chap. v.
[2] Nat. Indus. Conf. Board, Research Report No. 21.

3

a fairly standardized form of employee representation through shop committees. It is the purpose of this chapter to set forth the fundamental features of the shop committee as found in those plans most recently instituted as well as those which have functioned for a longer period.

The two fundamental characteristics of the modern shop committee are, (1) the single council or committee representing a single plant or industrial unit and (2) the use of the joint committee.[3] The plans set up by the National War Labor Board and the majority of those established within the last three years have been based upon the single plant council composed of representatives of the employees and an equal or less number of representatives of the management. The idea of a bicameral body, embodied in the early Leitch plans and modeled after the legislative organization of a political state, has not prevailed. The principle of the joint committee is practically common to all the most important plans of shop committees now in use.[4]

The Joint Shop Committee.—The Joint Shop Committee, as worked out by the various industries, presents two distinct types. First, there is the Single Works Council, composed of equal numbers of representatives from employees and management, the agency for collective dealing for the whole plant. Where the Single Council is very large, many plans provide for the appointment of a smaller Executive Council. The Main Council further expedites its work by appointing subcommittees, permanent and temporary. This form is found especially in small establishments and in large industries with small compact units. Where the industry is small the representatives are simply elected at large, but in the majority of cases there is a division of the plant into voting units, sections or departments. The Industrial Councils, set up by

---

[3] " The Joint meeting is the characteristic thing about the shop committee form of industrial government. It is more than characteristic, it is fundamental. The entire purpose of shop committee systems is to bring employer and employee together, face to face " (Stoddard, The Shop Committee, p. 28).

[4] Cf. A. B. Wolfe, report, Works Committees and Joint Industrial Councils, p. 92.

the International Harvester Company in March 1919, provided for a single joint Works Council for each plant, elected from departments:

"The Works Council at each plant is equally composed of representatives, freely and secretly nominated and elected by the employees, with voting divisions so arranged as to give due representation to all crafts and shop areas, and of representatives appointed by the management." [5]

The Goodyear Tire and Rubber Company divided its plant into forty voting precincts, each of which elects a member to the House of Representatives.[6] The number of representatives elected from the voting divisions varies among the several plants, depending upon the size of the plant and upon the size of the Council. Representation from the various departments is generally worked out on a numerical basis. Among the more important plans based upon a single Works Council elected from voting divisions or departments are those of the Bethlehem Steel Corporation, the Youngstown Sheet and Tube Company, and the Willys-Overland Company.

The second type of the Joint Shop Council is based upon a system of joint divisional committees, which,[7] although subordinate to the General Joint Committee, are nevertheless functioning units in the scheme of collective negotiation. The extension of the shop committee to large industries has been responsible for the increased use of the departmental or divisional committee. The National War Labor Board proceeded upon the principle that committees representing a shop, department or division of a plant should be the foundation of a shop committee system. In such an arrangement, there is a division of labor; matters which affect the particular division are discussed by the local joint committee for that

---

[5] Address of A. H. Young, "Industrial Cooperation," Chicago, Oct. 16, 1919.
[6] Bulletin of Goodyear Tire and Rubber Co.
[7] Not all local or departmental committees are joint. Many plans have shop or divisional committees composed only of employee representatives, but provide for calling of joint committees at stated intervals or as occasion arises. Wolfe, p. 168. Cf. Plan of Bethlehem Steel Corporation.

division, and only matters affecting the entire plant come under the scope of the general committee.

Some of the largest and most recent systems have been based on departmental or divisional committees. The plans installed by the War Labor Board in the forty or more plants coming under the Bridgeport Award provided for a General Plant Committee, supported by a system of divisional or sectional committees. The system employed by the Philadelphia Rapid Transit Company is based upon Joint Branch Committees which in turn form joint Departmental Committees, which in turn elect from their number members of the General Committee. The Constitution of the Plan of Representation for the Employees of Armour and Company provides as follows: [8]

(1) There shall be organized, at each plant where the size and local conditions of the plant warrant it,—
(a) Divisional Committees and
(b) Plant Conference Board.
After stipulating the divisions into which the plant is to be divided, Sec. 3, Art. 2 provides:—
(3) For convenience in holding elections and to secure broad representation of all employees, the above divisions shall be divided into voting precincts. From these voting precincts, the employees shall elect representatives to serve on the divisional committees and also on the Plant Conference Board. These precincts may be adjusted or changed from time to time, to secure fair and complete representation.
(4) The Divisional Committees shall comprise representatives from the employees within the division, and an equal number of representatives of the management.
(5) The Plant Conference Board shall comprise representatives of the plant as a whole and an equal number of representatives of the management.

The shop committee system of the Standard Oil Company of New Jersey is a system of Works Councils based on Divisional committees. [9] The plan of employee representation recently established by the Pennsylvania Railroad provides for a series of local, section or divisional committees, leading up to the General Joint Council for the entire system. [10]

---

[8] Plan of Representation for the Employees of Armour and Company, adopted Aug. 1921.
[9] Bulletin issued by Industrial Relations Department of the Standard Oil Co. of New Jersey. New York City.
[10] Railway Age, July 2, 1921, p. 14.

Composition of the General Joint Committee.—It is interesting as well as significant to note the variety of methods employed in the formation of the General Works Committee. As noted above, those systems functioning by means of but a single Joint Shop Council may elect the members either at large or from various departments, divisions or voting units; but with those systems involving a scheme of divisional or departmental committees, the problem is more complex and involves to a greater degree the question of just representation.

Under the War Labor Board Plans the members of the local or divisional committees formed the General Joint Committee. Where this resulted in too cumbersome a body for efficiency, the Central Committee might be composed of the Chairmen of the departmental committees as provided for in the Bridgeport plans. Under this scheme the divisional representatives act in a dual capacity, as representatives of their local division and as members of the main Works Council representing the whole plant. It has come to be the general opinion, however, that the interests of justice and fair dealing are best served where members of the departmental committees are not allowed to act as general committeemen.[11] Very often the central body is forced to act as a court of appeals for the lower committees. Again, it should be as free as possible from sectional or group bias. The more up-to-date plans have provided, in one way or another, for a Central Council distinct in personnel from the local committees. The General Committee of the Lynn Plan was elected from the employees at large by the members of the divisional committees especially convened for that purpose. Under the Armour Plan of shop committees, in all plants having more than six hundred and fifty employees, the "employee members of the Plant Conference Board shall be elected under the same conditions and at the same time as the employee members of the Divisional Committees." "An employee cannot serve as a representative on both the Divisional Committee

---

[11] Stoddard, The Shop Committee, p. 36.

and the Conference Board. If nominated for both, he must make his choice as to which office he will accept." [12]

The General Joint Conference.—In most of the plans instituted in large corporations with two or more units, there is provision for a general joint conference representing the entire organization. Its date of meeting may be fixed or conditional. In the majority of plans there is provision for a definite annual or semi-annual conference of all the employee representatives with all the representatives of the management. The plan of the Colorado Fuel and Iron Company provides definitely for the Annual Joint Meeting of all the representatives from the mines, camps and mills, to agree on the new contract and to discuss matters of mutual concern.[13] The shop committee representatives of the five works of the Standard Oil Company of New Jersey meet annually with the officials of the Company where matters affecting the whole industry are discussed and adjusted. The General Councils of the International Harvester Company may be called by the president whenever he considers the questions involved as affecting more than one plant. The provisions for a General Conference Board in the Armour Plan are illuminating:

(1) Whenever in the opinion of the General Superintendent any matter coming before any Plant Conference Board affects other plants of the Company, or whenever he desires to refer any matter as provided in the preceding section, he may call a General Conference Board to consider such matter, and thereafter the Plant Conference Board shall take no further action thereon.

(2) The General Conference Board shall be formed in the following manner; the General Superintendent shall issue a notice designating the several plants which he deems jointly interested. Thereupon, the Employee Representatives in the Plant Conference Boards at each of the plants designated shall select a representative or representatives from their own number to act as members of the General Conference Board. There shall be one such member of the General Conference Board for the firsts one thousand or less employees in any plant, and one additional member for each additional one thousand employees or major fraction thereof. These representatives shall be elected specially for each General Conference Board and their terms of office will expire at the end of such meeting.

Bases of Representation.—As pointed out above, the modern shop committee involves a division of the plant into sec-

---

[12] Armour Plan of Representation, Section of art. 2.
[13] Description of plan in King, Industry and Humanity, pp. 434–448.

tions, districts, or departments, either as voting units or as the bases for local committees. The difficulty of a proper and just classification of the employees increases with the size of the plant. The majority of shop committee systems use a division based on one of four principles or a combination of several. There is first, the craft basis; second, divisions based upon functional units; third, the geographical basis; and fourth, representation on a plain numerical basis.

The voting divisions of the International Harvester Company are so arranged as to give "due representation to all crafts and shop areas." The shop committee system of the Standard Oil Company divides each refinery into divisions, corresponding as closely as possible to the craft organization existing in the plant. The Lynn Plan, a War Labor Board system, secured a classification on a combination of the craft and the geographical basis. In transportation systems the trend is for a division along a geographical basis such as the regional districts of the Pennsylvania Railroad, or a functional division, as the Joint Committees of the Philadelphia Rapid Transit Company, which correspond to five operating departments of the company. In all the plans there is a numerical basis of representation, largely influenced by the size of the plant and the working limits of a committee. The number of employees allotted a single representative range from fifty in small plants, up to three hundred in the larger companies. The numerical limitation applies only to the local or divisional committees.

Elections.—The rules and regulations governing elections under the shop committee are set forth in great detail in the various constitutions. The majority of the plans provide for annual elections, held during working hours within the plant, and supervised by the General Joint Committee or a joint committee especially appointed for that purpose. It is usually stipulated that the elections shall be by secret ballot.

The qualifications required of those who vote for employee representatives are equally exact. The International Harvester Company, the Standard Oil Company, and the Colorado Fuel and Iron Company place no restrictions upon the suffrage save that all employees having the power of employment or discharge, such as foremen, assistant foremen and head clerks, are not permitted to vote for employee representatives. Other companies require a certain term of service, a certain age, or both, as qualifications for voting. The Youngstown Sheet and Tube Company requires sixty days prior employment and an age of eighteen years or over. Another plan limits the right of voting and of holding office to wage earning employees who have been three months in the service of the company. The provision of the Armour Plan is representative of modern systems:

> All hourly paid employees over 18 years of age, both men and women shall be entitled to vote, provided they have been in the service of the company for thirty (30) days immediately prior to the election. Steady time employees, such as Foremen, Assistant Foremen, Clerks, Timekeepers, and employees having the power of supervision and employment shall not be entitled to vote.[14]

Representatives.—The representatives, both of the men and of the management, occupy a strategic position in the modern shop committee. Those of the management are generally appointed by the employer and are chosen from all employees above the rank of wage earners. The management often appoints a special representative who gives his full time to the work and represents the management in all matters relating to the labor policies and in its dealings with committees of employees. Such a representative is often chosen to preside over the General Joint Committee representing the entire works. He is variously known as Labor Manager, Manager of Industrial Relations or as the President's Industrial Representative. Such an official is provided for in the plans of the Colorado Fuel and Iron Company, the Standard Oil Company, and the International Harvester Company.

The requirements demanded of employee representatives are more strict than those for voting and are set forth with great care. Eligibility for holding office as an employee representative may include a specified term of previous service

---

[14] Constitution of Armour Plan, art. 4, sec. 1.

with the company, American citizenship or at least first papers, educational requirements such as ability to read and write the English language, and a definite age minimum. The Harvester Plan, which has been the model for numerous other systems, provides that " None but citizens of the country, 21 years of age or over, and having had at least a year of company service are eligible as employee representatives." The stipulations of the Armour Plan are similar, with the further provision limiting representatives of precincts or divisions to employees of those areas. The Bridgeport Plan requires merely three months' previous service, the Philadelphia Rapid Transit Company requires a previous service of two years. A requirement of from six months to a year of previous service, coupled with American citizenship, is a common practice.

The majority of shop committee plans provide for an annual election of representatives. There are few restrictions against a representative serving more than one term, and under most plans he might be returned to office as often as his constituency desired. For some special committees, such as the General Joint Conference Board of the Armour Plan, the terms of the representative expire with the adjournment of that particular committee. The employee representatives of Proctor and Gamble are elected for two years, one-half of the representatives changing each year.[15]

Provision for recall of employee representatives is a feature of shop committee plans. On petition of the members of a division or department, an election may be held and the representative of that department recalled by a two-thirds vote or by a certain stipulated majority. Under the Harvester Plan, "Any employee representative may be recalled by majority petition and majority vote of his constituents." The provisions of the Armour Plan are typical of the rules governing recall found in a large number of shop committees:

Whenever a petition is filed with the Chairman of the Conference Board, signed by not less than one-third of eligible votes of a precinct or division, asking for the recall of their representatives, a

---

[15] National Industrial Conference Board, Research Report No. 21.

special election by secret ballot shall be held in that precinct or division under the direction of the Conference Board to decide whether such representative shall be recalled or continued in office.

If at such an election a majority of the employees in the precinct or division vote in favor of recalling their representative, then his term of office shall immediately cease; otherwise he shall continue in office.

Among the shop committees providing for a recall of employee representatives are included the committees set up at Bridgeport by the War Labor Board, those of the Bethlehem Steel Company, the Youngstown Sheet and Tube Company, the Midvale Steel and Ordnance Company, and the General Electric Company.

A number of shop committee systems include as a feature a definite guarantee of the independence of action of the employee representative, with provisions for his protection against discrimination because of activities in the line of his duties. He is either granted the right of appeal to the executives of the company or to outside arbitration. The Harvester Plan provides for both.[16] The Armour Plan gives to employee representatives the right to appeal directly to the Superintendent, and from him to the General Superintendent. There is no provision for outside arbitration. In the majority of plans, the representative has the same recourse in case of a grievance as that open to the individual employee and provided by the shop committee system.

Meetings.—Under a system of shop committees, definite provision is made for meetings of the committees or the joint conferences of representatives. The regulations of most plans prescribe in detail with reference to the time, place and frequency of meetings, their rules of procedure, and compensation for time spent by employee representatives in such meetings.

As in the case of other features of the shop committee, no uniform practice with respect to the holding of meetings is

---

[16] "The independence of every employee representative in his actions is guaranteed by providing for direct appeal to the President of the company in case that he believes that he is being discriminated against in his employment because of his conduct as an employee representative; and if he is not satisfied with the President's disposition of the appeal, he may ask and shall immediately secure impartial outside arbitration."

found among the various systems.   The most prominent
plans provide for regular meetings, with special meetings of
committees called as need arises.   In the vast majority of
plans the Works Council or General Joint Committee representing the entire plant must meet at a regular interval, in
most cases at least once a month.   Special meetings of the
Works Council may be called by the Chairman or by a number of members as need arises.   The meetings of the divisional committees may or may not be regular.   In most cases
they are called as occasion arises.   The Works Councils of
the Harvester Plan must meet once a month and may meet
as much oftener as they see fit.   The provisions of the
Armour Plan as to meetings are as follows:

Each Divisional Committee shall hold regular monthly meetings at
times fixed by it.   Special meetings may be called by the Chairman,
or any three members of the Committees upon application to the
Secretary, whenever necessary; sub-committees shall meet whenever
necessary.
The Plant Conference Board shall hold regular monthly meetings;
special meetings may be held upon call of the Chairman, or upon
application of any three members of the Board.[17]

The idea of regular meetings of the committees at stated
intervals, with provision for special meetings as occasion
arises is firmly fixed in the American shop committee.   By
this means there is always at hand the machinery for permanent and continuous negotiation between management and
men.

Full provision is made for the complete organization of
both the departmental committees and for a procedure strictly
in accord with parliamentary rules.   Each committee has its
Chairman, Secretary and necessary subordinate officers.   The
Chairmen of divisional committees may be selected in a number of ways, elected by the Committee or appointed by the
management.   The position of Chairman of a Plant or General Council requires an exceptional degree of training and
judgment and is usually filled by an appointee of the management.   The proceedings of all committees are carefully re-

---

[17] Constitution of Plan of Employee Representation of Armour &
Co.

corded and copies filed with the management and circulated among the employees. It is a common requirement that all business of special cases be submitted to the committees in writing, together with the names of witnesses and notation of fact bearing upon the cases. The committees are generally invested with power to summon witnesses, hear testimony and make personal investigation. The powers of the Harvester Councils are particularly full. They may " summon any employee as a witness and may secure from the management any information required in its deliberations; . . . may visit any part of the plant as a body or by committee." [18] Where the committee has under consideration a grievance, its deliberations take on the forms of court procedure; in the consideration of policies, its activities are those of a legislative assembly.

The meetings of committees are held, for the most part, on company time, in rooms specially prepared for the purpose in the plant. A few plans provide for meetings outside working hours. Under most plans there is provision for compensation to representatives for the time spent in committee activities, either by the company or by the employees. Each employee representative is paid in proportion to his earnings had he been engaged in his usual work. In a large number of plans, the whole expense of the committee organization is borne by the company.[19] The Armour Plan provides that suitable places of meetings shall be furnished at the Company's expense, that employee representatives shall receive regular pay from the Company during service on committees, and that in addition to this the representatives of both employees and management serving on the General Conference Boards shall receive reasonable traveling expenses, including hotel bills. The provision of the International Harvester Company as to this is as follows:

" The company pays employees for time lost from work while acting as employee representatives or service as witness

---

[18] Address of A. H. Young, Industrial Cooperation.
[19] Plan of Colorado Fuel & Iron Co.

before the council, but the employees may, if they choose, compensate such employees by pro-rata subscription among themselves."

Methods of Procedure.—The operation of the shop committee and the procedure followed by it must now be examined. In essence it partakes of the character of a system of government based on a series of committees with varying degrees of authority culminating in one joint supreme council.[20] Questions involving a dispute or grievance on the part of employees are first taken up by the local representative or sectional committee and may be carried to the supreme joint council for adjustment. Policies or proposals of the management affecting the entire plant are submitted to the joint council for negotiation. Suggestions made by employees are acted on by the general works committee or are committed to an appropriate standing committee for investigation and report to the supreme body. The work of the executive is lodged in the hands of the management.

Since a large part of the work of shop committees consists in the adjustment of disputes and differences between employees, between employees and foremen and between foremen, the procedure involved is clearly defined in the rules of the various plans. In general it is required that any employee having a grievance shall first bring it to the attention of his representative who in turn takes it up with the foreman or brings it before the sectional committee for adjustment. Failing of settlement here, the matter may come before a higher official of the company, from whose decision there is provided an appeal to a higher joint committee or to the central council representing the entire plant. From this body the matter may come before a special conference or be submitted to the chief executive for his final decision. There may or may not be provision for arbitration by neutral parties and unless such provision is made, the executive has the final

---

[20] There are various forms of settlement: by negotiation, joint meetings, joint councils, and special adjustment committees. Nat. Ind. Conf. Board, Research Report No. 21, pp. 33–43.

decision in the matter.   The purpose of such a procedure is to settle as many differences as possible by immediate conference between the parties concerned and to prevent them from coming before the general joint committee.   The provision for an orderly process of appeal leaves the way always open for a peaceable settlement of problems as they arise.

The course of procedure provided in the Lynn Plan is illustrative of the general type of procedure used in the plans installed under the supervision of the National War Labor Board.[21]   The employee representatives of each section constituted a Committee of Fair Dealing and the individual employee having a grievance had the right to take it up either with his foreman or with his representatives.   If the foreman or representatives failed to effect settlement, the case was to be presented in writing to the Joint Shop Committee, composed of representative groups of sections.   From here the matter might be taken to the Manufacturing Engineer of the head of the department involved.   Still failing of settlement the question might then be referred to the General Joint Committee on Adjustment for action and report to the management.   In case this Committee failed to reach a decision the matter was to be referred to the management for final adjustment.   A satisfactory settlement to the employee concerned or a unanimous decision of a joint committee at any stage of the proceedings was considered as final and binding, leaving no right of further appeal.

Under the Harvester Council Plan, any employee or group of employees may present suggestions, requests or complaints directly to the Works Council, either through the Secretary or through any employee representative.   An appeal is provided from the decision of the Council to the President of the Company.   The procedure set forth under the Armour Plan of Committees is more complex, based as it is on a series of committees.   Quoting from the Constitution:

Employees desiring to bring any matters before the Divisional Committees of the Plant Conference Board, may present them to the Employment Superintendent, either in person or through their precinct

---

[21] Stoddard, The Shop Committee, pp. 48–54.

representatives. It shall be his duty first to ascertain whether or not the matter has been properly presented to the Department Superintendent, and if not, he shall see that this is promptly done. If the matter cannot be adjusted by the Department Superintendent, the Employment Superintendent shall then present it to the Divisional Committee for their action. If not then disposed of by the Divisional Committee he will then present it to the Plant Conference Board for their action. Special meetings may be called to give early consideration to important matters or they may be carried over to the next regular meeting.

The provisions in most plans for hearing witnesses, making investigations, and securing evidence are most ample. Employees are granted the right to appear in person before committees, or groups may select individuals from their own number to represent them. Where it is thought necessary the deliberations of the committees may be in private. In most well-organized systems, testimony is recorded and full minutes kept of transactions. Petitions, recommendations and reports are usually required to be made in writing.

Voting in Joint Committees.—The method of voting used in the final determination of matters is an important feature of the shop committee. In practice a wide variety of methods are found, ranging from a simple majority of the joint committee to a unanimous vote.[22] In general, however, there may be said to be but two outstanding methods of arriving at a final determination; one that of a vote by a certain stipulated majority, two-thirds or three-fourths, and second that of the unanimous vote under the unit plan. The Bridgeport committees were required to reach a decision by a majority of two votes in a committee of six, or a five-sixths majority. The Harvester plan, the Philadelphia Rapid Transit plan and the Armour plan all require a unanimous decision, each group, employer and employee retiring before voting and casting the group vote as a unit. It is a common provision, under such plans, that both the employees and the employers shall have the right to withdraw temporarily from a meeting for private discussion. The rules governing the final vote and committee procedure of the Armour plan are typical:

---

[22] The decisions of the Joint Committee of the Colorado Fuel & Iron Co. are by a simple majority vote of the whole committee.

After complete investigation and full discussion of any matter under consideration by the Divisional Committees or Conference Board, the Chairman shall call for a vote which shall be secret, unless otherwise provided by the Board. The Employee Representatives and the Management Representatives shall vote separately. The vote of the majority of the Employee Representatives shall be taken as the vote of all and recorded as their unit vote. Similarly, the vote of a majority of the Management Representatives shall be taken as the vote of all and recorded as their unit vote.

Both the Employee Representatives, and the Management Representatives shall have the right to withdraw temporarily from any meeting, for private discussion of any matter under consideration.

In case of a tie vote in the Divisional Committees or Conference Board, it shall be in order to re-open the discussion, to offer a substitute or compromise recommendation, on which the vote shall be taken in the same manner as above provided.

Once the joint committee, general or special, to which a dispute has been referred, has arrived at a decision by the constitutional means, its decision is accepted as final and binding upon both parties. Where the committee has been unable to arrive at a decision, the procedure varies among the different plans. Some make no provision at all for a deadlock save that of reconsideration. Others, like the Standard Oil Company plan, provide an appeal from the Executive Council of a plant to the higher officials of the Company, who have final and binding decision. In such cases, failure of the joint committees to effect settlement throws the matter into the hands of the management without chance of further appeal.

Arbitration.—The provision for ultimate settlement by means of neutral, compulsory arbitration is a common feature of the largest and most recent forms of the shop committee. The provisions for arbitration contained in the plan of the Colorado Fuel and Iron Company are especially full and ample. Following a futile appeal to the President of the Company, any employee, through his representative, may request an appeal, or the President may voluntarily refer the difference, to the Joint Committee on Industrial Cooperation and Conciliation of the District involved. Here the matter may either be settled by majority vote or through the services of an umpire called in by majority vote of the Joint Committee. In the event of failure by either of these methods, the parties to the dispute have the final choice of two courses.

Upon agreement of the parties involved, the matter may be referred to arbitration, either by one arbitrator or by a board of three arbitrators, one to be selected by the Employee Representatives on the District Committee, one by the representatives of the Company and a third by the two already selected. The alternative course is an appeal, by consent of the District Joint Committee, to the Industrial Commission of the State of Colorado, which may be asked either to appoint a board of arbitration or to adjudicate the matter itself. The decision of any Board to which the matter has been definitely committed is binding on both Company and men.

The Philadelphia Rapid Transit Company provides for arbitration in the case of a deadlock in the General Joint Committee. Without choice on the part of either party, inability to come to an agreement is followed by the selection of the Board of Arbitration. It is composed of three men, one chosen by the employee general committee, one by the employer's general committee and a third by the two already selected. In case the first fail to agree upon a third, the Provost of the University of Pennsylvania, the Chairman of the Public Service Commission and the President of the Chamber of Commerce, or their representatives, are requested to act, thus increasing the Board of Arbitration to five. In the absence of a unanimous decision, the findings of any three shall be considered binding on both Company and men.

Among other prominent shop committee systems provided with arbitration features are included those of the Youngstown Sheet and Tube Company, the Midvale Steel and Ordnance Company, the International Harvester Company and the recent plan of Armour and Company. The last two provide for calling a general council from all the plants of the company and an attempt by this general council to reach a settlement, before resort is had to arbitration. In both cases the matter may be submitted only to impartial arbitration by mutual agreement of the parties concerned.

Scope of Committees.—The range of matters submitted to shop committees for action is an important and final con-

4

sideration. In this respect a wide variety is found in existing systems. The matters dealt with under the plan and the
degree of control over them depend upon what has been stipulated in the constitution of the committee system. Some
plans provide only for the adjustment of grievances; others
commit to the care of shop committees the welfare work of
the plant, together with the safety work, the health and sanitation work and benefit and insurance associations. A third
group of plans deal with wages, hours and working conditions and still others include questions of shop discipline and
management.

The full-fledged shop committee, truly representative of
the existing American type, deals with all four of these as-
pects of labor relations. The Harvester Works Councils will
hear "any suggestion, request or complaint, pertaining to
wages, hours, working conditions, recreation, education or
any other matter of mutual interest." The Constitution of
the Armour Plan provides:

> The Plant Conference Board and the Divisional Committees, may
> consider and make recommendation on all questions related to—
> > Employment and Working Conditions
> > Wages and Cost of Living
> > Safety and Prevention of Accidents
> > Health and Plant Sanitation
> > Hours of Labor
> > Education and Publications
> > Recreation and Athletics
> > Other Matters of Mutual Interest.

With respect to matters of shop discipline, hiring, promotion and discharge, there is a much greater difference of
opinion and practice. One investigation revealed seventy-
three Works Councils which dealt with shop discipline, discharge or promotion or both,[23] as follows:

> Of these seventy-three Works Councils, thirty deal with both
> matters, while seventeen deal with hiring, promotion and discharge,
> and twenty-six with shop discipline alone. Hiring, promotion, and
> discharge, is therefore, taken up by forty-seven Works Councils, and
> shop discipline by fifty-six. Field investigation disclosed that in many
> cases in which these matters were mentioned among the activities of
> Works Councils, the function was exercised as one of review and
> recommendation only.

[23] National Industrial Conference Board, Research Report No. 21,
p. 29.

On the other hand, several of the larger plans expressly exclude such matters from consideration by shop committees. Among such plans are those of the Youngstown Sheet and Tube Company, the Colorado Fuel and Iron Company and the Davis Coal and Coke Company. The provision in the constitution of the Colorado Fuel and Iron Company plan is typical: " The right to hire and discharge, the management of the properties, and the direction of the working forces, shall be vested exclusively in the Company, and except as expressly restricted, this right shall not be abridged by anything contained therein."

In general it may be said that the modern and standard shop committee deals with all questions arising out of the terms of employment, such as hours, wages and working conditions, and all other matters of mutual interest to management and men in their relation as employer and employee. Rarely do the shop committees concern themselves with questions of management or higher plant policy. The large majority of shop committee systems are likewise charged with welfare work such as housing, education and restrooms, lunchrooms, and medical aid. Under " Working Conditions " shop committees also deal with safety work and factory sanitation and hygiene. However, the true sphere of a shop committee system, whatever else may be committed to it, is that of wages, hours and working conditions of the employees. So widely is this recognized that any plan which excludes such matters from the consideration of its committees, is spoken of as a " limited plan."

A word might be said in conclusion with respect to the degree of authority allowed to shop committees regarding the extent to which, at least in theory, they actually share in management. The powers exercised by the committees are legislative and judicial; the executive power remains in the hands of the management. The work of the joint committees has to do with policies and principles; the responsibility for carrying out these policies lies solely with the management.[24] Good faith on the part of the management requires that the decision of a joint committee in any matter which is within its proper jurisdiction should be accepted and carried out. Failure of a joint committee to agree results in one of two courses. The matter may go to the manager or chief executive, who has the veto power and whose decision is final and binding. In this case joint control ceases with the failure of the joint shop committee to agree. The alternative is recourse to impartial arbitration, in which case there is a sacrifice of control on the part of the management to the extent of an agreement to abide by the decision of the arbitration board.

Thus it cannot be said that the shop committee implies industrial democracy. Its limitations must be clearly understood. The control of the employer over the general management problems such as sales, finance, production and choice of personnel are complete. Some control has been given to shop committees, in a few cases, of plant discipline. The functions of the shop committees are limited to the problems arising out of the relations between employer and employee. Even in this sphere joint control may be exercised up to a certain point only. The determination of the limits of joint control is, in the long run, in the hands of the human factors themselves, and depends to a large degree on their will to cooperate.

---

[24] " The plan definitely states it to be the province of the Works Councils to determine the policy of the Company with reference to matters of mutual interest. That policy having been determined, its execution lies wholly with the management. However, any question as to the manner of execution again lies within the jurisdiction of the Council. In other words, the legislative and judicial functions are on a fifty-fifty basis, but the executive power still lies wholly with the management " (The Harvester Plan, an address on " Industrial Cooperation," by Arthur H. Young, of International Harvester Co., given in Chicago, Oct. 16, 1919).

CHAPTER III

The Shop Committee in Operation

In the last chapter the shop committee was analyzed as to its form and organization. In brief, it amounts to a compact system for joint dealings between the men and management of a single corporation or business establishment. There is no provision for association with other shop committees in the same industry. It permits no representation of employees or employer save by representatives chosen from within the organization. The employees are not organized primarily to exert economic pressure. The agreements arrived at as to wages, working conditions and other matters of mutual interest to management and men apply strictly to the industry concerned. Where joint negotiations fail there is usually a provision for some form of arbitration, ultimately by outside or neutral parties. The shop committee is not primarily a workers' organization; nor is it an employers' organization. It is a form of joint organization for the individual plant whereby the labor problems of the plant are governed by collective negotiations through joint committees composed of representatives of men and management.

The workings of the shop committee cannot be studied from the standpoint of a system of collective bargaining. The shop committee, confessedly, is not such a system. Its advantages, if any, must be found in its application to the problems of the individual industrial establishment. Whatever defects it may be found to possess, must lie in its working in this same field. The actual value of the shop committee will be found only by an examination of its operation as a system of local shop government and not as a fully developed system of collective bargaining. We are examining, therefore, the shop committee, viewed as a system for collective dealing centering in the individual corporation.

53

The performance of the shop committees set up by the National War Labor Board has already been noted. Yet it must be pointed out that the experience of the shop committees during the war period is not an adequate test, nor does it furnish grounds for sound conclusions. The plans were in many instances forced upon reluctant employers, accepted by indifferent employees, and supported all along by the powers of the various government war labor agencies. The real test of the shop committee has been its experience during the last four years. It is from the working of the shop committee in these years following the war that the soundest conclusions as to its value may be drawn.

Before going into a detailed analysis of the operation of the shop committee, three general observations must be noted, revealed by the history of the last four years. In the first place, the shop committee invariably receives its initial impetus from the employer. The large majority of the plans set up within the last three years have been initiated by the management and accepted by the men.[1] There is first the formal announcement by the company of their intention or willingness to organize shop committees. A general plan is formulated by the management and submitted to the men for their adoption or rejection. Rejection by the men is almost always followed by the abandonment of the plan and a return to whatever conditions previously existed. Where the men signify their willingness to accept the plan, they are requested to elect representatives to a joint drafting committee which proceeds to work out the plan of representation in detail. This, having been again approved by a general election of the employees and passed on by the Board of Directors, becomes the working constitution for the plant. Committees are then elected under its provisions.

In the second place, the shop committee has shown itself

---

[1] The writer knows of but one plan set up at the request of employees. The plan of Employee Representation of the Tide Water Oil Company, Bayonne, N. J., was inaugurated on the demand of employees who asked for a plan similar to the one operating in the Standard Oil Company of New Jersey.

sensible to the fluctuations in industry. Figures quoted from a recent investigation of the shop committee show that it is found for the most part in industries employing relatively large numbers of men.[2] In a number of shop committees recently abandoned, the reason assigned was the shutting down of the plant or the reduction of the working force.[3] One plant reported that a reduction of the force to one-twelfth of its normal strength was the prime cause in the permanent lapse of the plan.[4] The hope was expressed that with the return of business activity, the shop committee might be restored. The reduction in the number of the working force also renders it much easier to maintain a close touch between the management and the men.[5] With the increase of the working force, the shop committee would again be needed to facilitate this function.

In the third place, the continuous existence of the shop committee is never assured. The ease of its installation is equalled only by the ease of its rejection. While in most cases there is a provision for the repeal of the plan at the option of either party six months or a year after its initial adoption, as a matter of fact shop committees may lapse or be abandoned from a number of reasons. Several plans have failed or have simply vanished from lack of sufficient interest on the part of the employees.[6] Again the employer is responsible for the abolition of the system, letting it lapse from

---

[2] National Industrial Conference Board, Research Reports 21-31, p. 15.

[3] The committees of one company were abandoned during the summer of 1920 when, " due to business conditions it was necessary for us to materially reduce our force, consequently, many members of the various department committees left our employ." Quoted from a letter written by officials of the company.

[4] Plan of Bath Iron Works, Ltd., Bath, Me.

[5] Holt Mfg. Co., Peoria, Ill. " We do not have a shop committee now, as our present personnel is less than 25% of our normal working force, and contact with this small group is so close and intimate that there is no real need of any form of employee representation." Letter.

[6] One plan was abandoned by the employees on a motion of the employee representative who said: " Let us quit this boy's play and adjourn to the time when the president will call us together and have something to say " (" Industry," a bulletin issued by Associated Industries of Massachusetts, vol. ii, No. 12, p. 1).

inactivity. While the birth of the shop committee may cause quite a stir in the plant, its death may occasion not even a ripple, save on the rare occasion when it is the result of a violent struggle with the union.

This last consideration has an important bearing upon the question, Is the shop committee a success? It cannot be answered for shop committees in general. Each shop committee system must be considered as a case by itself, and since its life is so uncertain, its very existence depends upon its success. The fact of survival implies satisfaction. No plan has any chance to survive that is not mutually satisfactory to the parties concerned. The majority of the shop committees existing at present owe their very existence to the fact that they are alive, active, and are performing the functions for which they were set up. A study of the shop committee is therefore a study of the shop committee at its best, for at its worst it does not exist. Given a reasonable period of trial, the shop committee either languishes and peacefully disappears, or develops strength and flourishes.

A survey of the operation of shop committees shows that their activities may be grouped under four main heads:

(1) Wages, hours and other terms of employment.
(2) Adjustment of grievances and complaints.
(3) Production.
(4) Living and working conditions.

Wages, Hours and Other Terms of Employment.—In the matter of wages and hours the shop committees have shown a marked degree of activity, technique and success. The capacity of the shop committee to formulate wage scales was amply demonstrated by its experience under the National War Labor Board. That it has continued to function in this capacity is borne out by a review of its operation in the existing shop committee systems. It may be safely said that the majority of shop committees have to do actively with the adjustment and negotiation of wages, hours and working schedules.[7]   The experience of the Bridgeport Brass Company is typical.   In 1919, out of a total of two hundred and forty-eight meetings of shop committees, thirty-seven or fifteen per cent were devoted to the consideration of wages and working conditions.   In 1920 thirteen per cent of the meetings were for the purpose of making wage adjustments.   " Taking the wage scale at the time of the adoption of the plan as one hundred it has since been increased to one hundred and sixteen per cent, and now stands [8] at eighty-seven per cent of this basis.   These changes have been worked out in a manner acceptable to the joint committees of employers and employees representatives." [9]   During the first fifteen months of the plan set up by the Standard Oil Company of New Jersey, ninety-four Joint Conferences were held at the five refineries. Of the total of one hundred and forty-one matters discussed, wages and hours amounted to forty-four and four-tenths per cent.[10]   Among the accomplishments credited by President Grace to the shop committees of the Bethlehem Steel Company are, first, the adjustment of numerous wage and piece rates, second, adjustments in the schedule of working hours, and, third, the adoption of more uniform pay periods and better methods of paying off.[11]   The shop council of the Elgin National Watch Company, at the suggestion of the management, took under advisement a system of profit-sharing and after careful study and discussion decided not to urge its adoption.[12]

The readjustments of wages necessitated by the business depression of 1919–1920 offered test of the ability of the shop committee to handle the problems of wage reductions.

[7] The National Industrial Board found in their investigation that out of a total of 225 Works Councils, 145 were expressly reported as dealing with wages, hours, and working schedules.   Research Report No. 21, Oct. 1919, p. 67.

[8] January 1922.

[9] Letter from the Company, January 27, 1922.

[10] Bulletin of the Personnel Department of the Standard Oil Co. of N. J.

[11] Printed letter from the Bethlehem Steel Co., Oct. 1921.

[12] Second Annual Report of the Chairman of the Elgin National Watch Co. Employees' Advisory Council, p. 6.

Many of the plants so reducing wages, announced in connection that it had been done through the agency of the shop committee. In addition to the plans already referred to, the Walworth Manufacturing Company, the Lynn plant of the General Electric Company, the McCallum Hosiery Company, and the International Harvester Company used their shop committees in making wage reductions and readjustments. According to their testimony they have been able to reduce wages and to readjust rates in keeping with the industrial depression and the reduced cost of living with the consent and cooperation of the workers, and without the slightest friction.[13]

The experience of these shop committees in handling proposals for the reduction of wages is illuminating as to the working of the shop committee system of collective dealing. Early in December 1920, one plant found itself under the necessity of reducing the price of its finished product. The President of the Company went before the shop committee and informed the members of the coming reduction of twenty-five per cent in prices. No reduction in wages was asked for, but instead the employees were asked by the Company to appoint a committee from their number to investigate the cost of living in their city. If, however, the employees were convinced by their investigation that the cost of living had gone down, they would be asked to accept a reduction in wages to correspond with that decrease. In January of 1921 the committee reported a decrease of eighteen per cent in the cost of living, a finding that agreed with the results of a similar investigation made by the Company's Personnel Department. The facts were submitted to the whole shop committee who after discussion agreed to accept a reduction of from ten to fifteen per cent in their wages.[14]

The announcement by the International Harvester Company that wages and hours would be determined by the

---

[13] Bulletin No. 12 of the Associated Industries of Mass., p. 2.
[14] From a report of the President of the Walworth Mfg. Co., submitted to a Conference of the Associated Industries of Mass., Bulletin No. 13, p. 1.

Works Council was the signal in several plants for immediate demands for higher wages and shorter hours. The management, through its representatives, presented their case to the Works Council. " We were able to show that our wages and rates were as high or higher than in similar industries in our vicinity, and that only through constructive work in the Council, through greater efficiency in the reduction of costs would we be enabled to pay higher wages and still remain in a competitive market; . . ." [15] As a result of discussions in the joint committee, with but one exception the demands were voluntarily withdrawn by the employee representatives. Since that occasion, general increases of wages have been negotiated by all the Works Councils.

This process of collective dealing on the matter of wages and hours and the opportunity given for the exchange of ideas and propositions is illustrated by the account of the wage reduction carried out by the Colorado Fuel and Iron Company early in 1921. The Company became desirous of reducing the costs of their products and decided to lay the facts before the employees' representatives.

This was done at the annual joint meeting of representatives and officials at Pueblo, December 11. On January 4, at the meeting of the Steel Works representatives, the Company officials still further reviewed business conditions and the needs for reduced costs stating that in addition to economies that could be secured by other means, they believed a reduction of twenty per cent in the wages of steel workers was necessary.

The employees' representatives later consulted their respective constituencies and on the second day following, again met the officials. At this meeting the employees' representatives read a resolution, which they had previously passed in a meeting by themselves, proposing a reduction of fifteen per cent in wages. The employees in the plant authorized their representatives to assure the officials that they would endeavor by greater effort and greater economies to make up the difference of the remaining five per cent in the management's original proposal. This offer was accepted by the officials, and although there were no orders in hand for wire and nails, they promised the representatives that under this arrangement operations at the wire department would be resumed at a moderate rate, and that portion of the product which could not be shipped promptly would be put into stock.[16]

---

[15] Testimony of the Manager of Industrial Relations for the Harvester Co. Address in Chicago, Oct. 16, 1919.
[16] The Colorado Fuel and Iron Industrial Bulletin, Jan. 21, 1921.

Under the head of wages and working conditions, the shop committees have been called upon to handle many allied problems such as strikes and reduction of the working force. In one instance [17] the Works Councils were empowered by the management to determine whether the plants would be closed down because of a strike in another plant and, being closed down by order of the shop committee, when they would resume operations. The Company claimed to have been very well satisfied with the handling of the situation by the shop committee. In another instance the employee representatives on the joint shop committee upheld their right to be consulted with respect to lay-offs due to reduction of the working forces.[18] Many of the questions as to wages arise as the result of protests from individuals or departments. The shop committee has been able to handle these as they arise without waiting for any stipulated time for discussions as to the general wage scale.

Three features of this aspect of collective dealing may be pointed out. In the first place, the demands of any group of workmen for increases in wages must of necessity meet with the approval of their fellow workmen; otherwise they cannot win the support of their representatives and have little chance of success in the shop committee.[19] In the second place, the employee representatives are enabled to keep in close touch with the wishes of their constituencies by means of special meetings and conferences. Before being required to give answer to proposals made by employers in the meetings of the joint committee, the employee representatives are afforded ample time and opportunity to consult the employees. The agreements of the representatives, therefore, as a rule, represent the opinion of the mass of employees and are supported as such. In the last place, the management has taken advantage of the joint committees to present all the information

---

[17] The Steel Strike in one plant of the International Harvester Co.
[18] Proceedings of the Deering Works Council meeting, The Deering Main Wheel, Dec. 1920.
[19] More than one instance has been noted where the demands of groups of employees for higher wages failed because they did not meet the approval of the employee representatives.

and reasons for proposals put forward. The state of the business, production costs, the net earnings of the company and sales data are presented as considerations for a reduction or increase in wages. As a result, the agreements reached are taken in a better spirit by both parties than the arbitrary posting of a wage scale without warning or opportunity for discussion.

Grievances.—One of the most important forms of shop committee activity is found in the consideration and adjustment of grievances. One investigator found that the greatest value of the shop committee to a certain company was its efficiency as a medium for bringing small and immediate grievances to the attention of the company.[20] Many of the disputes never come before the shop committees for adjustment but are settled through the offices of the employee representatives. Under the plans, there is every evidence that the employees felt the fullest freedom in bringing their slightest complaint for adjustment. Statistics on this matter are difficult to obtain but such as are available show the extent to which the shop committees function in the adjustment of complaints. The results achieved by one company under this plan are set forth by the General Manager.[21] In the first year of the plan, out of one thousand two hundred cases, one thousand and twenty were "adjusted satisfactorily without action by the shop committees, but as a result of the plan of representation." In two years two hundred and ninety-eight cases reached the shop committees for action.

Thirty per cent were settled unanimously in favor of the employee and one and a half per cent were settled in his favor by majority decisions; forty-one per cent were settled unanimously against the employee; fourteen per cent were withdrawn; three and a half per cent were settled in the employee's favor by the Adjustment Committee and five and a half per cent were settled against him. Only three cases out of the two hundred and ninety-eight brought before the shop committees in two years got as far as the Manager. . . .

[20] Special report by A. H. Lichty on the Works Councils of the Harvester Co.
[21] Testimony of Richard H. Rice, General Manager of the Lynn Works of the General Electric Co., Bulletin of the Associated Industries of Mass., June 4, 1921.

The shop committees of the Bethlehem Steel Company, during a period of three years, considered and settled to the mutual satisfaction of both the employees' representatives and the management over one thousand four hundred and sixty cases.[22]

It is interesting to note the nature of the complaints that come before the representatives or before the joint committees for action.   At first glance the majority of cases appear really vested with an importance not to be ignored.   They concern the intimate details of shop life, petty personal relations and in most cases grievances that would never have come to light had the opportunity not existed through the employee representatives and the various shop committees. In most cases, left unadjusted, they would have led to serious trouble or at least would have formed the basis for secret grudges, ill-will and eventual separation from the company.

A review of the minutes of one of these joint shop committees is typical of numerous other meetings of similar character.   The following are the complaints and action taken by a typical shop committee meeting : [23]

Complaint : Employees of the No. 1 foundry requested that a storm shed be installed at the south end of the foundry near the office to eliminate the draft.

Action : This shed was ordered installed.

Complaint : Employees in paint department complained that draft from the bridge between buildings 29 and 21, fourth floor, causes considerable sickness.

Action : Committee recommended that swinging doors be installed.

Complaint : No drinking facilities in the stock department.

Action : Committee ordered drinking fountain installed.

Complaints as to the inadequacy of safety devices are numerous.   Many of the most important grievances have to do with questions of discharge.   The following instance is typical : a mechanic was discharged by his foreman because he had left his tool chest unlocked and some one had stolen his

---

[22] Bulletin of the Bethlehem Steel Co., Oct. 1921.
[23] Deering Works Council Proceedings, Dec. 3, 1920.

tools. The employee protested that he had locked his chest in the proper manner but that the lock had later been broken by an accident and that he was in no way to blame. The foreman remained unconvinced and the man, through his representative, appealed his case to the shop committee. Here, before a joint committee, evidence was brought to light which supported the employee and resulted in his reinstatement. As the result of an investigation covering the nineteen Shop Councils of the Harvester Company the uncovering of grievances and the provisions for adjustment was given as one of the most important functions of the shop committees.[24]

Production.—An examination of the activities of various shop committees shows a third function not so widespread as the first two but important for its possibilities. This is the time devoted by a few shop committees to the consideration of shop efficiency and economies in production. The employees, through their representatives, are encouraged to make suggestions as to efficiency or better methods of production. This activity has been noted as assisting the company in making better promotions and in discovering good material among their employees.[25] Statistics obtained from one company show the extent to which employees have used the shop committees to voice their ideas on production and efficiency.[26] In 1919 nine per cent of the meetings were devoted to the subject of plant economies; in 1920, ten per cent. An officer of the Company says: " during the last two years, three hundred and twenty-eight suggestions for economies and improvements in manufacturing equipment and methods have been submitted, of which twenty-eight per cent have been adopted by the management."[27] This form of activity is to be found in only a very small minority of the shop committee systems in existence. In October 1919, the National Industrial Conference Board reported: " The participation of

[24] A. H. Lichty, Special report to the President on the Works Councils of the International Harvester Co.
[25] Ibid.
[26] Bridgeport Brass Co.
[27] Letter of January 27, 1922.

Works Councils in the elimination of wasteful methods and in the improvement of industrial equipment and process has been relatively infrequent." [28]   There has been no marked change in this condition in the last three years.   Such instances as are found of this activity are evidence of potential capacity rather than universal practice.

Living and Working Conditions.—The fourth function of the shop committees has been found to lie in a field, the importance of which has been steadily increasing.   This field has commonly been described under the term "welfare," which, owing to the peculiar odium attached to it by groups of workers, and to the implication of paternalism, has become increasingly objectionable.   A more appropriate as well as a more accurate description of the activities referred to is found in the phrase "Living and Working Conditions."   The National Industrial Conference Board has arranged these activities under two main heads: first, Social and Recreational Activities; and second, Living and Working Conditions.   Living and Working Conditions are divided by the report into three parts:

(1) Social Welfare of Employees, such as housing, cooperative stores, medical aid, insurance, education and Americanization.

(2) Industrial Betterment in the Plant, such as first-aid service, rest rooms, lunch rooms, and prizes, etc.

(3) Working Conditions in the Plant, such as accident prevention, factory sanitation and hygiene.

There seems to be no special reason for making Social and Recreational Activities a division by itself, for logically such activities come under the head of the Social Welfare of Employees.   All the activities mentioned properly come under the head of Living and Working Conditions, for in the words of the report, "they concern those interests, apart from hours of work, and wages, which affect the welfare and life of the employees of an individual establishment." [29]

---

[28] Research Report No. 21, p. 73.
[29] Ibid., p. 59.

It was in this field of activities that employees, even before the advent of the shop committee or the trade union got their first share of control and participation. In many cases the existence of safety committees, cooperative stores committees, athletic committees and mutual benefit associations, composed for the most part of employees, were the stimulus and starting point for the organization of a shop committee system. In many cases the experience and knowledge gained from them played a large part in the successful operation by employees of the shop committees. It is only natural, therefore, to find that the modern shop committees are concerned to a very great extent with the consideration and even conduct of these activities.

The Report mentioned above [30] notes that three-fourths of all the Works Councils established on the initiative of employers concern themselves with one or more of these matters. The relative importance of Living and Working Conditions in the work of the shop committees may be judged from the actual experience of several of the most successful systems. In the first fifteen months of the existence of the shop committees of the Standard Oil Company, thirty per cent of the topics handled had to do with sanitation, housing, social and miscellaneous items. Among the most important of the accomplishments of the shop committees of the Bethlehem Steel Company the following items are listed:

(1) Inaugurating a plan of acquainting the new employees, not only with their job, but also with the provisions of the plan of representation by instruction through the foreman.

(2) Institution of Plant Schools during working hours for non-English speaking employees.

(3) Recommendation of a Savings Plan through periodical pay deductions which resulted in the adoption of the plan for the purchase of Victory Notes.

(4) Studied and recommended a plan for Employees' Relief Association which was adopted and installed.

(5) Secured many improvements in safety devices and

[30] Ibid.

5

lighting facilities, installation of washroom, shower bath, toilet and locker accommodations and drinking fountains.[31]

In 1919, sixty-three per cent of the meetings of the shop committees of the Bridgeport Brass Company were held for the purpose of taking action on Living and Working Conditions, which included Disability and Life Insurance, Safety and Sanitation, Athletics and Recreation, Americanization and Education. In 1920, seventy-four per cent of the meetings were devoted to such activities. The table given below shows the proportion relative to the other activities of the committees : [32]

COMPARATIVE TABULATION OF NUMBER AND PURPOSE
OF
INDUSTRIAL COOPERATIVE RELATIONS MEETINGS HELD DURING
1919–1920

	1919		1920	
1. Disability and Life Insurance.......	32	13%	38	17%
2. Safety and Sanitation.............	27	11%	23	10.5%
3. Athletic and Recreation...........	76	30.5%	80	36.5%
4. Americanization and Education.....	23	9%	21	10%
5. Wages and Working Conditions.....	37	15%	29	13%
6. Plant Economies.................	22	9%	21	10%
7. Miscellaneous...................	31	12.5%	7	3%
8. Total........................	248	100%	219	100%

These matters having to do with Living and Working Conditions are handled by the shop committees in a variety of ways. In some plans, as in the Harvester Plan, they are discussed in the Works Councils, the joint shop committee for a single plant. In others, as in the plan of the Colorado Fuel and Iron Company, there are special or standing committees having these matters in hand. Three of the permanent Joint District Committees of the Colorado Fuel and Iron Plan are concerned with Living and Working Conditions: the Joint Committee on Safety and Accidents, the Joint Committee on Sanitation, Health and Housing, and the Joint Committee on

---

[31] Pamphlet issued by President Grace of the Bethlehem Steel Co., Oct. 1921.
[32] Bridgeport Brass Co.

Recreation and Education.   In others, these matters as they arise are referred to sub-committees appointed especially for the particular occasion.   In all of these plans, such matters can and do continually arise in the nature of grievances or conflicts and as such may come before the highest joint committee in the shop. .

There is little doubt but that the employees have shown a very marked degree of interest in the management and control of Living and Working Conditions through the shop committees.   Undoubtedly the degree of success attained by the shop committees is due in large measure to the fact that they have opened up to the individual employee an opportunity for a real share in the initiation, control and management of these activities having to do with his living and working conditions.   The interest of the employee in the management of mutual benefit associations, in the inauguration of savings campaigns, in the conduct of cooperative stores and housing projects and in the improvement of the safety and sanitary conditions of his shop life, appears in many instances to overshadow his interest in management, industrial control and even in the wage policy.   He is much more interested in his own opportunity to have a voice in the management of these affairs of immediate concern to him, than in being properly represented at a National Conference of his Industry or in having a seat on the Board of Directors of his corporation.

Type of Representatives.—Turning from an analysis of the functions of the shop committees, we must criticize certain of their features in the light of experience.   One of the most important factors in the working of shop committees is the type of representatives chosen by the employees.   In the first place, in the majority of plans the employee representatives have been workmen of more than average intelligence, of long experience in their respective shops and of eminently conservative attitude.   One observer, commenting on the elections of four hundred and twenty-two departmental committees under his supervision, noted that the employees usually elected were of long service and apparently of a set and conservative character.[33]   The average length of service of members of the executive committees of the Locomobile, Remington Typewriter, Singer and U. M. C. factories in Bridgeport, Connecticut, was a little more than seven years. The chairman of these four joint committees had an average service record of thirteen years. A conference of executives experienced in the operation of shop committees expressed the opinion that " it appeared to be the general experience that when radicals among the workers are elected to the shop committees they soon become conservative."[34]   There has been a prevailing feeling of confidence among executives in the ability of employee representatives to deal fairly and render sound decisions.[35]   In contrast to this view, one case was found where the plan failed, owing to the weakness and incapacity of the representatives chosen. One investigation pointed out that the failure of the employees to elect strong men as representatives was a weakness of the plan concerned.[36]

There are, however, strong grounds for feeling that the limitations on the choice of employee representatives in the modern shop committee are a serious defect. In most plans, the employee representatives are elected only for short terms, annually or semi-annually. Many of the Committees formed for special work are composed of representatives who serve only for the duration of that particular emergency. There is no opportunity here to acquire experience through long service similar to that acquired by the company representatives. It is true that representatives are eligible for reëlection and that many representatives do acquire a certain experience and skill from continued service. On the other hand it has been pointed out that this advantage may be offset by a high labor turnover. A more serious obstacle lies in the fact that the employee representative is required to serve in addition to his

[33] Stoddard, The Shop Committee.
[34] Bulletin of Associated Industries of Mass., May 28, 1921, p. 2.
[35] Testimony of General Manager of the Lynn Works of the General Electric Co., Industry, p. 2.
[36] Cited in Bulletin of the Associated Industries of Mass., June 4, 1921, p. 4.

regular duties in the factory. Mr. Lichty, in the personal investigation referred to above, found that this was one of the commonest complaints of the employee representatives themselves. One employee representative, a member of the union, asserted that representatives were tied down to their work so closely that they couldn't make satisfactory investigations.[37] He suggested that the employees should have at least one full-time representative of their own. Another employee representative testified that he had great difficulty in finding time to look after the work of the Council.

While it is, no doubt, highly desirable that the majority of representatives should be elected at stated intervals from the body of workmen in the shop, it seems that there is need of a few or at least one representative from the employees, who has had special training and experience and who is free to devote his whole time to the work as representative. One shop committee, in fact, has such a representative. The chairman of the shop committee of the Nunn, Bush & Weldon Shoe Company of Milwaukee, Wisconsin, is elected and paid by the employees. He devotes all his time to making personal investigations, adjusting grievances, and presiding at the meetings.[38] The spread of this feature to the rest of the shop committees is highly desirable and would tend to increase its value as a system of collective dealing for employees.

Problem of Meetings.—The shop committee has revealed a second weakness in its operation. Two complaints have been lodged by employees and investigators against the system of shop committee meetings. In the first place, in some instances the shop committees have been slow in their action on matters referred to them and the delay has caused irritation and dissatisfaction. The main criticism directed against one plan was the absence of despatch in attending to its business. It was urged that a speeding up of the action of the Works Councils was a necessity if the plan was to enjoy full success.

---

[37] Special Report of A. H. Lichty, cited above.
[38] Commons, Industrial Government, pp. 125-134.

A second criticism, allied to the first, is that there is not sufficient freedom in the calling of meetings of the shop committees.   In most plans the meetings of the committee are at
stated intervals.   In the case of a matter arising, requiring
immediate action, it must wait until the next regular meeting
of the committee for action.   It has been pointed out that the
employees' representatives should be given greater freedom
in calling special meetings to handle matters as they arise.[39]
This would make for speedier action and would increase the
efficiency of the shop committees in the adjustment of grievances.   In these matters promptness is the first requisite to
successful treatment.

In justice to the shop committee, however, it must be noted
that collective dealing through the joint committees has, in
the large majority of cases, been successful.   In spite of the
limitations on the selection of employee representatives and
of the handicaps under which they function; in spite of weaknesses in the committee system itself; the vast majority of
shop committee meetings are marked by orderly procedure,
unrestricted discussion and a final action mutually satisfactory to both parties.[40]   In the vast majority of instances the
recommendations of the employee committees or the joint
committees are adopted and acted upon by the management.
The experience of one company over a period of two years is
typical: "nearly seventy per cent of all the disputes brought
to the table were settled wholly as requested by the workmen
delegates; twenty-eight per cent were settled by both sides
taking an even compromise and two per cent were lost by the
employees, who abided by the decision." [41]   There is scarcely
a record of a joint committee meeting that broke up in a
wrangle.   It has been estimated that "out of the thousands
of disputes that have been discussed at the council meetings

[39] Testimony of former employee representative, Colorado Fuel
and Iron Co., in Industrial Bulletin, April 1920, p. 5.
[40] Summary of Conference Reports on Employee Representation
Plans, Bulletin of the Associated Industries of Mass., June 4, 1921,
p. 1.
[41] Employee Representation, Success or Failure, Outlook, Aug. 31,
1921, p. 689.

attended by equal representation of the management and workers, over ninety-four per cent of the cases have been settled to the entire satisfaction of both management and men at the conference table, six per cent have gone up to the final council, and five and three-quarters per cent of those cases were settled without going to the President's table or to the impartial arbitration board." [42]   The few cases in which arbitration has been resorted to is a dominant fact of shop committee experience.   The joint conference has demonstrated its effectiveness in collective dealings both involving the adjustment of local disputes and the consideration of matters of production and living and working conditions.

Beneficial Contributions of Shop Committee.—From an analysis of shop committee experience and from the testimony of employees and employers participating in this form of collective dealing, certain benefits stand out as positive contributions of the shop committee to industrial relations. As has been pointed out, they have to do solely with the relations between management and men within the individual plant or establishment.

There is first the improvement in discipline.   There was formerly a tendency of foremen and executives to fear that the shop committee would undermine the control of the foreman over his men.   This has not been borne out by experience.[43]   The relief from the arbitrary rulings of the management and the opening of an avenue of appeal from the arrogance of foremen has been a decided benefit to the men.[44] Under a system of shop committees, foremen are less likely to provoke trouble without reason, knowing that their conduct is subject to a public review before a joint committee.   Employees are less ready to bring unreasonable and unjustified

---

[42] Outlook, Aug. 31, 1921, p. 689.   In one plant during 2 years, of the 298 cases brought before the General Joint Committee, all but 3 were satisfactorily adjusted without appeal to the Manager.   Testimony of the General Manager of the Lynn Plant of the General Electric Co., Bulletin of the Associated Industries of Mass., June 4, 1921.

[43] Associated Industries of Mass., Bulletin No. 13, p. 1.

[44] Special Report of A. H. Lichty.

complaints for the same reason.   One of the benefits enu-
merated as a result of one detailed investigation was that the
members of the management were not so hasty or arbitrary
as before the introduction of the shop committees.[45]   Employees have testified to the beneficial effect of such a system
on discipline in their shop.[46]

A second benefit, ranking in importance with the first, is
the value of the system in uncovering grievances and in providing a method for prompt adjustment.   This has been
pointed out time and again by both management and men.
The settlement of these grievances without stoppage of work
is also considered a valuable feature of the system.   An employee representative of one plant, a member of the union,
asserted that in these matters the plan got more details attended to and was a greater help than the union.[47]

A third benefit of the shop committee is the opportunity it
gives for the management to learn the desires and needs of
the men and for the men to learn of the problems of management and condition of the company.   This is preëminently
the mutual educational feature of the system of regular collective dealing.   The committees are often used by the management to discuss the state of the business and to refute
false rumors of enormous profits.   Through petitions from
the men the management is often informed of conditions of
which they had been in total ignorance.   This mutual give
and take is one of the most beneficial features of shop committee dealings.   The almost universal testimony of executives who have had any dealings at all with shop committees
is that the joint committees' meetings are responsible for
bringing about a better relation and a more sympathetic feeling between management and men.   That this increase of

---

[45] Ibid.

[46] Ibid.   One management representative of the South Chicago
Works of the International Harvester Co. testified that the shop
councils had enforced, not weakened, the control of the management.

[47] Special Report of A. H. Lichty, Benham Works.

good will has resulted in increased production is a common observation.[48]

In the fourth place, the share in the control of benefit activities of the establishment, opened to the employee through the shop committee, is a decided contribution to labor relations in the plant. It seems to satisfy, to a marked degree, the desire of the average employee for a recognition of his ability and initiative. It gives him an active interest in addition to his job. The ability to get immediate action, through the committees, in matters affecting his personal comfort in the work shop or activities outside of working hours, is greatly prized by the individual employee. It has had no little place in winning his interest in the shop committee. The first activities of newly installed shop committees most often have to do with the improvement of working conditions, safety, and sanitation.

The shop committee has shown its ability to interest all classes of employees, union as well as non-union workmen. In several instances where the plan was adopted by only part of the plant, it has been extended at the request of employees who originally opposed it.[49] The participation of union men in the shop committees is especially worthy of note. In the Harvester Company about half of the one hundred and seventy-five employee representatives were listed as union men.[50] In another the number of union men acting as employee representatives was in 1919 ninety-nine and nine-tenths per cent. In 1921 the number was given as about fifty per cent. The testimony of union representatives gives some light on the attitude of union men towards the shop committee. One union representative, a member of the Brotherhood of Locomotive Engineers, though that " in time it will make

---

[48] General Conclusions of the Special Investigation made by A. H. Lichty.

[49] Two plants of the International Harvester Co., which had refused to accept the Council Plan when first presented and later asked to reconsider their decision, voted to accept the Plan.

[50] The joint shop committee system was extended at the request of the employees of the Standard Oil Co. of N. J., to several new departments of the corporation.

the union unnecessary." In one company the union representatives testified that the plan suited the men better than the union, giving as their reasons, (1) no strikes, (2) no dues, and (3) better control over their actions.[51] In the main, however, union men, even though favorable to the shop committee and cooperating in its operation, retain their membership in the union. Their reasons for this have been stated by one authority in industrial relations as follows: first, they may leave the employ of the company and their union membership might be of service to them elsewhere; and second, they sincerely believe that the ideals of trade unionism are sound and valuable.[52]

The shop committee has likewise obtained a strong place with employers. It may safely be asserted that the large majority of employers who have had experience with shop committees are favorably impressed. The summary of the Report on Works Councils in the United States by the National Industrial Conference Board stated: "Approximately three-fourths of the employers having Works Councils from whom an expression of opinion was secured, declared themselves in favor of this form of industrial organization or that their experience had been favorable."[53] At a Conference of New England industrial managers and executives last May, the shop committee was given strong endorsement. "In general it was the testimony of the speakers that employee representation had brought the employers and employees closer together . . . removing causes for misunderstanding and making for more harmonious relations."[54]

The President's Second Industrial Conference devoted much time to the examination of shop committee employee representation. In conclusion it said: "The Conference has had the benefit of testimony from both employers and employees who have had experience of the results of employee

---

[51] Special Investigation, A. H. Lichty.
[52] Personal letter to the writer from a manager of industrial relations of a large corporation.
[53] Research Report No. 21.
[54] Bulletin of Associated Industries of Mass., No. 12.

representation.   An enthusiasm has been shown which comes from a sincere feeling of substantial progress in the development of human relations." [55]

In conclusion then, the operation of the shop committee is found to center around individual plant or corporation.   Its defects and advantages are those of a system of industrial relations having to do solely with the shop or plant as the industrial unit.   It is, moreover, a system which does not survive unless it works.   The continuous existence of a shop committee is a guarantee of its success.

The most important activities of shop committees have to do with four principal phases of the local labor relation:

(1) Wages, hours and other conditions of employment.

(2) Adjustment of grievances and the consideration of complaints.

(3) Cooperation in production.

(4) Discussion and management of activities having to do with living and working conditions, in and outside of the shop.

There are two weaknesses in this system of collective dealing through joint committees.   One is the limitations on the choice of employee representatives.   The operation of the plan would be strengthened by the provision for one or more full-time employee representatives, chosen either from among the employees or from the outside, but who shall give their full time to that particular plant.   The second is the lack of flexibility in the provision for meetings.   The value and effectiveness of the plan would be greatly improved by a greater freedom to call meetings to handle grievances as they arise.

However, in spite of the handicaps under which the workmen representatives function, the meetings of the joint committees have been remarkably successful.   The majority of them reach satisfactory conclusions in an orderly manner, there is a mutual confidence in the sincerity of both parties, strikes and the appeal to outside arbitration are rare.   Plans

---

[55] Report of the Industrial Conference called by the President, March 6, 1920, p. 12.

in which the executive has attempted to over-ride or ignore the recommendations of his joint committees have invariably been unsuccessful. The willingness of the management to act sincerely on the recommendations of the joint committees is absolutely essential to the successful working of the shop committee system.

Finally, the burden of the evidence and testimony as to the results of the shop committee agree that it has made for a better relation between management and men. The most important factors making for this result are:

(1) The improvement in discipline.

(2) The prompt uncovering of grievances and their speedy adjustment.

(3) The mutual education of management and men through the system of regular collective dealings in the joint committees.

(4) The share in the management of living and working activities allowed to employees through their joint committees.

These contributions of the shop committee to the betterment of local labor relations may be said to be distinctive. They arise from the peculiar advantages of the shop committee itself and can be traced to no other source. To the extent that this observation is true, the shop committee has a place of its own in systems of industrial relations and must be taken into consideration when viewing the problems of labor as a whole.

CHAPTER IV

The Shop Committee and the Trade Uinon

The shop committee was first introduced into territory unorganized by the American trade unions. It was taken up largely by employers who either had never dealt with the unions, or who had successfully resisted all efforts to compel such dealings. Whatever may be said of the motives which prompted the introduction of the shop committee, it could hardly have been introduced as a substitute for the trade unions. In practically every instance, the shop committee brought to the workers their first opportunity to deal collectively with their employer. With a few exceptions [1] there were no open clashes between the shop committee and the unions. Actually, the two movements did not come in contact with each other. The official publications of the national trade unions had nothing to say.

The Whitley Report published by the British Ministry of Labor appeared early in 1917 with its advocacy of works councils and shop committees. In October of that year Samuel Gompers, President of the American Federation of Labor, wrote very favorably of its findings and recommendations, with special mention of the industrial statesmanship shown by its insistence upon the support and cooperation of trade unions in organizing the industrial councils and shop committees. [2]

---

[1] The shop committees set up in the Colorado Fuel and Iron Co., 1915, were viewed by the unions with suspicion and distrust. A leader of the mine workers is reported to have said at the time: "I am glad to assume that Mr. Rockefeller is earnest in his desire to do something for the miners but Mr. Rockefeller will be here only a week or two. After he is gone, what then? The miners will have neither organization nor contracts to protect them. They will be at the mercy of whatever superintendent or pit bosses the company may select" (New York Times, Sept. 23, 1915).

[2] American Federationist, Oct. 1917, p. 854.

The adoption and use of shop committees by the Government War Labor Agencies was received by the trade unions with conflicting attitudes. The Shipbuilding Labor Adjustment Board was the first to use the shop committees in its awards. Owing to the violent opposition of the local unions some of the shop committees were never set up and the operation of others was seriously handicapped. On the other hand the shop committee was used by the National War Labor Board with the full approval and cooperation of the trade union officials.[3] The decisions of the Board ordering the formation of shop committees in plants which had consistently refused to deal with the unions were especially pleasing to trade union officials.[4] In discussing the award of the National War Labor Board for the Bethlehem Steel Company ordering the installation of a shop committee system, Mr. Gompers said:

> Through assistance from the outside, the Bethlehem Steel workers may be able to make their shop committees the nucleus of an industrial constitution that will result in just as thorough an organization of that side of production in this plant which concerns employees as has existed on the side of the management. A shop committee for the Bethlehem Steel workers may mean the beginning of industrial freedom.
> The same benefits may be established for the workers in every other place where a shop committee is inaugurated; nor is it necessary to wait for an award from the War Labor Board. Shop committees can be established through the initiative of the workers themselves.[5]

In its report to the St. Paul Convention of the American Federation of Labor, held June 10, 1918, the Executive Council officially advocated the setting up of shop committees:

> The Executive Council believes that in all large permanent shops, a regular arrangement should be provided whereby;
> First, a committee of workers would regularly meet with the shop management to confer over matters of production; and whereby;
> Second, such committee could carry beyond the foreman and the superintendent, to the general manager or to the president, any important grievance which the workers may have with reference to wages, hours, and conditions.[6]

---

[3] Ibid., May 1918, p. 369.   Editorial.
[4] Ibid., May 1918.
[5] Ibid., Sept. 1918, p. 810.
[6] Ibid., July 1918, p. 581, Proceedings of the St. Paul Convention of the A. F. of L.

In discussing the Report of the British Ministry of Labor on " Works Committees," Mr. Gompers pointed out that the term " shop committee " as used by the National War Labor Board was practically synonymous with that of the British " works committee." [7] The general question of the relation, and the relative weight in power of works committees and trade unions would, in his estimation, be settled gradually through experience and the actual working out of the various systems. " But unless," he stated, " the works committee is properly related to and protected by trade unions, it cannot hope, in certain establishments at least, to discuss questions before the management with that sense of freedom which is essential to the success of joint deliberations."

> Where the workers have been trained in collective action, the shop committee will quickly become an effective machine, but where the workers have not had the experience of collective bargaining or trade union activity, the work of the shop committee is more difficult. . . . In order to protect these workers . . . the shop committees must be made strong, effective agencies. Trade unions should have an important part in accomplishing this purpose.[8]

The ready acquiescence of trade union leaders in the shop committees established by the National War Labor Board can be accounted for in a measure by the suppression of their right to push trade union organization during the war. Even so, the more serious and thoughtful of the trade union leaders saw in the shop committee favorable possibilities for labor in general. It was viewed first as a contribution to the machinery for securing industrial representation and for securing cooperation in production. In the second place, it offered to the large body of unorganized workers the chance to realize at least some of the advantages of organization and group action. In the third place, there was a definite feeling that the trade unions should include the shop committee in their programs and should seek to organize them in relation to the trade union movement. Finally, while it was admitted that shop committees alone were better than no representation at all, yet it was the conviction of trade union leaders that their

---

[7] Ibid., Sept. 1918, pp. 805–810.
[8] Ibid., p. 809.

full value could be secured and safeguarded only when functioning in relation to the trade union movement.

Could this attitude have prevailed and the two movements been permitted to work out their mutual relations gradually and sympathetically, the results might have been of untold value to industrial relations. The features of local autonomy characteristic of the shop committee might have softened the severity of employers' distaste to outside dictation by the " walking delegate." The trade union might have profited by the closer contact with shop conditions and have been influenced in favor of constructive policies, rather than the traditional policies of negation and restriction. To the shop committee would have been added a protective economic power and the broader scope of the national organization.

However, the intensity of the industrial conflict which ensued as soon as governmental control of industry was relinquished, prevented any peaceful evolution or gradual development. The radical element seeking to organize the steel industry forced the Atlantic City Convention to an open and complete denunciation of the shop committee and all similar systems of representation. The open shop drive of American employers, coupled with their announced intention of substituting the shop committee for the trade union, swept away any remaining obstacles to a complete break. The necessities of militant activity forced American trade unionism into an attitude of open antagonism and uncompromising hostility. The continuance of the struggle has only served to deepen the breech and to exaggerate the issues.

The first protests and keenest criticisms came from the rank and file of trade unionism. In their efforts to organize new fields they came into sharp conflict with the shop committee and the attitude of the trade union is clearly set forth as a result of these local encounters. William Z. Foster, a union organizer, gives his opinion of shop committee systems: [9]

---

[9] W. Z. Foster, The Great Steel Strike, p. 45. The reference here is to the shop committee plan of the Midvale Steel and Ordnance Co., set up by the National War Labor Board late in 1918.

Such company unions are invariably mere auxiliaries to the companies' labor-crushing systems. They serve to delude the workers into believing that they have some semblance of industrial democracy, and thus deter them from seeking the real thing. They consist merely of committees, made up for the most part of "hand-picked" bosses and "company suckers." There is no real organization of the workers. The men have no meetings off the property of the company; they lack the advice of skilled trade unionists; they have no funds or means to strike effectively; they are out of touch with the workers in other sections of the industry. Consequently they have neither opportunity to formulate their grievances nor power to enforce their adjustment. And little good would it do them if they had, for the "lick-spittle" committees are always careful to see that they handle no business unless it relates to "welfare work" or other comparatively insignificant matters.

Company unions are invariably contemptible. All of them are cursed with company dictation, and all of them lack the vivifying principles of democratic control.

The union committee in charge of the steel strike in the Colorado Fuel and Iron Company issued the following statement with reference to the company's plan of shop committee representation. First: "No collective bargaining exists under the Rockefeller plan, from a trade union standpoint." Second, in explanation of the eleventh demand of the unions which asked the abolition of company unions, the committee went on to say:

No more proof is needed to demonstrate that labor's future must be worked out for labor through its own trade union organization, directed by labor, without the patronage of employers' so-called "company unions."

Under the so-called "company plan," working conditions, hours, and wages are governed by their competitors in the steel industry. This makes the movement national in scope and we are compelled to stand squarely behind the twelve demands.[19]

When the strike was called off in January 1920, the men returning to work were required to sign a card, which among other things constituted an acknowledgment that the company operated under the Rockefeller Plan of Industrial Democracy. In March the union strike committee commented on the working of employee representation after the strike:

Union men have not displayed much interest in the election this year, although some changes are being made in the representation plan that will give the impression that the workers are getting shop

[19] Amalgamated Journal of Iron, Steel & Tin Workers, Mar. 11, 1920.

6

representation. The steel workers know from past experience that it is utterly impossible to get any consideration of their rights or wrongs under this paternal and autocratic institution.[11]

The unions repeatedly emphasized the point that the shop committees were lacking in economic power. One critic said:

> There has yet to appear the first employer or industrial-expert-made "industrial democracy" plan which contemplates the existence of trade union organizations as the expression of the workers' desires in the plant.
> There is present in every case subtle efforts to delude the workers into the belief that they are exercising a voice in industry, when as a matter of fact, the employer holds the veto and deciding power.
> Workers organized in trade unions need not accept without protest the arbitrary ruling of an employer. They have the means and the independence and the machinery with which to make effective protest.[12]

Commenting on the establishment of shop committees by the Western Union Telegraph Company, the union said: "The scheme was launched in this city and will have no more connection with the bona fide trade union movement than has Mr. Rockefeller's 'union' of Colorado miners."[13] The members of the machinists' union refused to cooperate in the shop committees set up in the United States Rock Island Arsenal: "The unionists now look upon this works council as the regulation 'company union.'"[14]

There are grounds for feeling that the officials of the American Federation of Labor, and especially Mr. Gompers, were slow to follow the wave of opposition to the shop committees. At least they were not quite ready to take a public stand against them. In fact Mr. Gompers gave to some of the members of the President's First Industrial Conference the impression that the A. F. of L. was not itself opposed to shop organization. It was only after he was directly challenged to explain the action of the Atlantic City Convention in condemning shop committees that he came out openly in opposition. He said:

---

[11] Ibid.
[12] Ibid., Sept. 1919, Editorial, "Quackery and Fakery."
[13] The Textile Worker, Oct. 1918.
[14] Amalgamated Journal, Sept. 9, 1920.

The declaration of the A. F. of L. resolution was the expression of its opinion and of its position, and undertakes to do what it could, and what it would, what I declare to this Conference, that we are going to keep the right of persuading and arguing in man fashion that those shop organizations shall be a thing of the past and that the bona fide organizations of men and women of labor shall take their places, where men and women can express themselves freely and uncontrolled except by their own conscience and judgment.[15]

Later in the conference Mr. Gompers said:

We believe that you are making a mistake by your shop organizations, the same as the mistake was made in England with the shop-steward method of organization, and which, by the way, has been discarded these several months, and there is scarcely a vestige of it left to tell the story that it existed.

We will not abandon the hope nor the effort to convert your shop organizations into union men and union women; but we will do it in our own fashion, our own manner, by persuasion, by intelligent argument, and presentation of experience to demonstrate to them that such an organization or system of organization is perversive of the interests of the wage workers and contrary to any spirit of manhood and independence.[16]

After declaring that the employers had definitely rejected the American Trade Union Movement, he said: " They want shop organizations, the employers' union. If they can get away with it, why that is their job, if they can; but they are building upon quicksand. They are resting their hope upon a flimsy ground and one which will not take long to turn upon them in their benevolent and solicitous attitude toward the workers in their employ." [17]

The question of the relation of the shop committee plan to the trade union movement was definitely made clear by the actions taken in the Montreal Convention of the American Federation of Labor, held in June 1920. Discussing the President's First Industrial Conference, the Report of the Executive Committee has the following to say:

The employers' delegation would not accept any resolution on collective bargaining unless it was so worded as to be anti-trade union in spirit and to provide encouragement and support for company unions. The position of the employers throughout the conference was a position of anti-unionism, a position of enmity and antagonism to

[15] Proceedings of the President's First Industrial Conference, p. 233.
[16] Ibid., p. 233.
[17] Ibid.

trade union effort and organization. . . . They sought continually to find a way to secure approval of the conference for various forms of shop and company organizations and the viewpoint which they sought constantly to inject was the viewpoint of the shop and the individual plant instead of the viewpoint of the industry as contemplated by the A. F. of L. and its affiliated organizations.[18]

The President's Second Industrial Conference in its recommendations had made much of the shop committee as a means of collective bargaining and had expressed the conviction that employee representation through shop committees was in no way incompatible with trade unionism. It made the assertion that shop committees had been found to operate with equal success both in union and non-union shops.[19] The Executive Committee of the A. F. of L. branded the work of the Conference as a failure and its findings as faulty in principle and impractical of application. It subjected the Conference to two criticisms:

(1) The attempt to impose a structure of artificial machinery upon the industrial system by law.

(2) It sought to " give encouragement and permanency to the various forms of company unions and shop organizations and various forms of so-called employee representation whose chief merit is that they serve the purpose of the employers by organizing the workers away from each other." [20]

The Executive Committee differed with the Conference in their conviction that shop committees and trade unionism went hand in hand. It said:

The Commission seems to view the problems of industry from the viewpoint of the single shop instead of from the viewpoint of industries. The character of American industry in its present stage of development and the work of the American trade union movement is ample proof of the fallacy of such a viewpoint. At the time this report is drafted no effort has been made to secure action in Congress toward setting up the machinery outlined by the President's Conference. Your Executive Committee is of the firm opinion that should an effort be made, Labor must exert every influence to encompass its defeat.[21]

[18] Proceedings of 40th Annual Convention of A. F. of L., June 1920, Report of Executive Committee, p. 83.
[19] Proceedings of President's Second Industrial Conference.
[20] Proceedings of Montreal Convention of A. F. of L., Executive Committee Report, p. 85.
[21] Ibid.

During the Convention, a resolution was unanimously passed condemning the shop committee plan of the Bell Telephone Company and empowering the American Federation of Labor and its affiliated organizations to oppose and resist by every means available the progress of all such schemes.[22]

The evidence leaves little doubt as to the present attitude of trade unionism towards the shop committee. Organized labor views the plan of representation through shop committees as contrary to the regular trade union movement both in principle and practice. The shop committee is a denial of the right of collective bargaining in the true meaning of the term; that is, the right of the worker to be represented by representatives of his own choosing, from whatever source. Among the charges brought against the shop committee by the trade union, there are five which may be said to stand out in importance as the reasons for trade union opposition.

First, the shop committee has become a device of the employer to defeat and supplant the modern trade union. The shop committee is synonymous with the open shop and for this reason alone, the merits of the plan, if any, must be disregarded and the whole force of organized labor lined up to oppose it.[23]

Second, the shop committee rests upon a faulty principle of organization. Building as it does upon the single plant as the real industrial unit, it ignores the industry as a whole, which is the unit recognized by organized labor. This tends to undermine the class loyalty of the worker and to weaken his bargaining power.

Third, the shop committee lacks any real economic power. The only protection of the worker lies in his own economic power and " in this vital respect, the company union is a complete failure. With hardly a pretense of organization, un-

---

[22] Ibid.

[23] Referring to the plan of representation proposed for the Pennsylvania Railroad, President Gompers said: " It all comes down to the fact that the proposal of General Atterbury is merely a subterfuge for the purpose of weakening the unions and lessening the ability of the workers to protect themselves " (American Federationist, July 1921).

affiliated with groups of workers in the same industry, destitute of funds and unfitted to use the strike weapon, it is totally unable to enforce its will, should it by a miracle have one . . . all it can do is to submit to the dictation of the company." [24]

Fourth, the shop committee fails to provide the worker with true representation. The workmen are limited in the choice of their representatives to those of their own number, employees of that particular company. This puts them invariably at a disadvantage in bargaining, because, denied the assistance of expert labor officials, they are no match for the representatives of the company.

Fifth, shop committee systems are convenient agencies for the exploitation, deception and oppression of the workers. Through such systems it is easier for an employee so willed to dictate, manipulate and control the wishes of his workers. The following practices have been charged at various times, as methods used to ham-string so-called democratic committee systems: [25]

(1) Unfair elections, loading of committees with bosses and uneven representation.

(2) No democratic organization permitted; shop committees are not allowed to meet independently and under their own control.

(3) Intimidation of committeemen through threat of discharge. Representatives have no protection in the disinterested discharge of their duties.

(4) Diversion of the aims of the workers by the company through leading discussions of committees from wages, hours and conditions to welfare plans, fake safety movements and vague problems of efficiency.

The policy, therefore, of modern trade unionism with reference to the shop committee is a logical outcome of its indictment against it. Any further growth of the shop committee

---

[24] American Federationist.
[25] Resolution adopted at the Atlantic City Convention of the A. F. of L.

must be opposed as a menace to the very existence of trade union collective bargaining. In plants where union men are working under the shop committee system, every effort must be made, by active opposition, by refusal to cooperate and by steady adverse propaganda, to defeat the successful administration of the plan and to accomplish its final abolition. This policy of opposition is based upon the conviction that there is no place in the present trade union organization for any of the ideas or machinery of shop committee representation; nor any common basis for harmonizing the two ideas. It is a case of one system in its entirety or of the other, and only the industrial struggle will determine which is to survive.

It cannot be denied that the position of trade unionism with reference to the shop committee is composed of elements of great strength. Its accusations are clearly based upon an understanding of the true nature of shop committee representation and are in the main founded on the facts of experience. On the other hand certain elements of weakness are present. In the first place, the condemnation of the shop committee by the trade union is partly the result of the instinct of self-preservation, a fear for the life of its own organization, which has prevented it from taking a broad view of the problems of labor. In many instances this has resulted in extreme views fostered by prejudice rather than reason, and in the exaggeration of many issues far above their real importance. In the second place, the policy followed by the trade unions is fraught with most serious consequences for both the shop committee and the trade unions. It may well be considered whether a modification of this attitude might not in the long run be for the best interests, not only of the American trade union movement but also of laboring men as a whole.

The arguments of the trade unions have been directed with unerring accuracy against the weakest points of the shop committee. In the first place, it cannot be denied that the shop committee has gained ground largely from the motive of the employer to head off trade union organization. Introduced at first almost without exception into open shop plants, the shop committee has been recently openly advocated and adopted in closed shops as a substitute for the prevailing system of trade union collective bargaining.   Such a tendency is most unfortunate,[26] especially from the standpoint of the shop committee, and to the extent that it does actually prevail, the trade unions are justified in viewing the shop committee as a menace to their organization.

In the second place, the emphasis of the shop committee upon the individual plant as the unit of industrial relations strikes at the heart of trade union philosophy, and the lack of a wider industrial or national basis has been noted as one of the chief defects of the shop committee as an instrument of employee representation.   The insistence on a horizontal cleavage of society, on the organization of workers as a class, and of employers as a class has been a characteristic of trade unionism both in England and in the United States.[27]   The modern trade union is unalterably opposed to any vertical cleavage which would tend to weaken the sense of class inter-dependence, destroy the power of labor for corporate self-help and cause a split in his loyalty.   A militant class union-ism could not but view with distrust the division of workers by shops and factories.   The absence of any organization covering the whole industry deprives the workers of protec-tion against a sweated industry.   As long as the shop com-mittee exists as a local organization, limited to the single establishment or corporation, the trades unions will be justi-fied in viewing it as an imperfect means of collective bar-gaining.

---

[26] " A greater danger than the temporary weakening of the workers' bargaining strength is the probability that, if the shop committee is used as a union substitute, the minds of the workers will become so inflamed that they will refuse to see its good points and will reject it utterly.   In other words, if it becomes a question of shop committee or trades-unionism, it will be the shop committees and not unionism that will ultimately disappear.   If the valuable possibilities of the shop committee are to be preserved, it must be clearly envisaged that it is to be a supplement to the union and not a substitute for them " (Paul H. Douglas, Journal of Political Economy, Feb. 1921, p. 103).

[27] Webb, Industrial Democracy.

In the third place, it cannot be doubted that compared with the trade union the shop committee is inferior in economic power. The unions cannot be blamed for their insistence on the importance of economic power to the workers. Neither public opinion nor the benevolence of the employer can be relied upon to protect the interests of the workers from the pressure of the modern industrial system. Experience has amply demonstrated that only by economic power have the workers secured a hearing and a fair bargaining position.

The shop committee is sadly deficient in this vital respect. It has no funds of its own, it is unaffiliated with other groups in the same industry, and by the very nature of its organization is totally unfitted to use the strike weapon. The unions are right in their belief that in the ability to exert effective economic pressure upon the employer, the shop committees are inferior to the modern national trade union.

Still, it may well be questioned whether the unions have not underestimated the real economic power of the shop committee. In several ways it is more peculiarly fitted to strike effectively than the trade union. Organized with the single plant or corporation as a unit, including in its membership all classes of employees, it is better able to paralyze completely the plant as a whole, than a union organized upon the basis of single trades or crafts. Although it has no strike funds and is incapable of a prolonged struggle, where the strike is so effective from the outset it lasts only a brief time. Where there is the will, the shop committee is fully able to wage a short, sharp struggle sufficiently effective to secure results. This has been demonstrated more than once in the history of the shop committee. One manager of industrial relations for a large corporation with twenty-one plants testified that under their plan of employee representation by joint shop committees, a strike would be infinitely more effective and more damaging than one instituted by the trade unions who could control only a portion of the men. The strike for higher wages instituted under the direction of the shop committee system of the Milwaukee Electric Railway completely paralyzed the company and achieved its purpose at the end of the first day.[28]

In view of these considerations, it would appear that the unions have exaggerated the lack of economic strength and that the shop committees are not exactly the helpless bodies they are represented to be. Admitting that the worker is not justified in giving up the strength residing in collective bargaining through the national trade union, still to many employees the shop committee is sufficiently strong for its purposes and offers features that more than compensate for a lack of superior economic power.[29] While the unions, therefore, rightly point out much that is lacking in the strength of the shop committees, they are not justified in the extreme position that they are totally lacking in this respect.

In charging that the shop committee does not guarantee the employee true representation, the unions are on firmer ground. The right to be represented implies a freedom of choice as to the means or instruments of representation.[30] The right to be represented by expert counsel in industrial negotiations is as valid as the right to be represented by expert legal counsel in a judicial proceeding. This has been recognized by both employers and unionists in all the experience of collective bargaining. The limitation of the choice of representatives in shop committee systems to the employees of the particular company is a limitation on the right of representation and a partial denial of what is professedly offered. This weakness of shop committee representation has been

---

[28] Commons, Industrial Government, p. 155.

[29] In this connection it may also be said that the shop committee is not primarily a militant organization. Its purpose is collective action in constructive matters as well as wages, working conditions, etc. Its spirit is cooperative, not combative. It may be questioned whether the constructive program of trade unions has not been seriously impaired by over-devotion to militant activities.

[30] "If the right of working men to be represented by representatives of their own choosing means anything, it must be a right unqualified by stipulations made by employers. Any limitation or restriction upon that right by employers destroys the right and removes from the workers the right to be represented by representatives of their own choosing" (Samuel Gompers, American Federationist, July 1921).

pointed out. While such representation is an improvement over individual bargaining and while much good has been accomplished under it, until the shop committee provides for the representation of the employees by experts of their own choosing, from whatever source derived, the trade unions will be justified in condemning it as imperfect and in standing out for representation of the workers in the true meaning of the term.

However, in their assertion that the shop committee is merely a convenient agency for the exploitation, deception and oppression of the worker, the basis for union opposition is weakest of all. In this argument more than in all the others the unions have been prone to misrepresentation and have been influenced by passion and prejudice. They have permitted observations undoubtedly true in a few instances to color their views of the whole field. The various practices which the unions assert are used to ham-string the democratic committees have been found only in a very small minority of cases and cannot be substantiated as the general rule. None of the abuses alleged by the unions is inherent in the shop committee itself. It is not true, for instance, that representatives in the normal representative shop committee have no protection in the disinterested discharge of their duties, or that unfair elections and "packed" committees are the rule.

It cannot be denied that where the employer is so willed, he can make the shop committee a fraud and employee representation a farce. Hardly any system of industrial relations is proof against ill-will and deliberate corruption. In this respect the trade unions are ill-qualified to throw stones at the shop committee. The employer determined to exploit his men has found a way, even with trade unions. Trade unions themselves do not wish to be judged by the worst unions, nor do trade union officials wish to be likened as a group to a Brindell. Neither should the unions have attempted to fasten upon the shop committee as a whole, the evil reputation created by its worst exhibits.

The unions have really underestimated the capacity of the American workman to detect deception and to protect himself from oppression.   The fact is, there is no one so quick to sense hypocrisy or to recognize and resent insincerity as the average workman.   Experience has amply demonstrated that no plan of shop committee which is not undertaken in full sincerity and in the spirit of cooperation has the least chance to survive.   Managers of industrial relations are practically a unit in warning employers that unless they are ready to cooperate sincerely on a square basis, they had better not take up the shop committee.

When seen at its best, the case of the trade union against the shop committee is expressed in the charge that it does not mean collective bargaining.   Added to this are, first, the inferior economic strength of the shop committee, second, its denial of true representation, third, the lack of a national basis for the organization.   The deficiencies of the shop committee very nearly correspond to the strongest features of trade unionism.

Admitting the general strength of the trade union position with respect to the shop committee, it remains to inquire as to the expediency of trade union policy.   Does the policy follow as a natural consequence of the views?   Granted that the shop committee is urged by employers as a substitute for trade unions, are the unions wise in opposing them, once they are installed?   Are the unions right in their view that they have nothing to gain from the shop committee and that there is no possible place for it in their organization?   It may well be considered whether the unions are not mistaken in their policy of uncompromising hostility.   There are, in fact, many grounds for the conviction that a moderation of this policy would be for the best interests, both of the shop committee and the trade union and ultimately for the general progress of industrial relations.

It must be pointed out in the first place, what seems to be an erroneous conception of the problem on the part of the unions.   The whole blame for extension of the shop committee has been placed upon the employer who has used it for setting up the open shop, with the intention of destroying the union. But the real problem of the union concerns itself with the workers. The real fact to be faced is that the shop committee idea has gained weight with large groups of employees, union as well as non-union. The battle is not so much between the unions and employers as between groups of employees. The opposition of the majority of modern employers to the trades unions can be taken for granted. An employer, the chances are, who insists upon collective dealings through shop committees could not be coerced to deal with the trade unions anyway; especially when his employees acquiesce in setting up the shop committee. As long as employers offer and their men accept the shop committee, it will supplant trade unionism.

The experience of the Pennsylvania Railroad with its shop committees during the shopmen's strike is illuminating on this point. The success of the Road in handling the strike was largely due to the loyalty of the majority of employees to their shop committees. The Railroad declared:

If a majority of the shop crafts were dissatisfied either with their wages and working conditions or with the methods of elections used by the Company, or with the proceedure adopted for the settlement of matters in dispute, no more propitious occasion for indicating such dissatisfaction could be presented than a strike by the shopmen all over the country.[31]

On the contrary, it is claimed by the Company that less than thirty per cent of its shopmen answered the strike call and in two months the shop forces had been recruited to ninety-five per cent of their normal number. Commenting on this, the Road says: "It would be difficult to imagine stronger proof of the fact that the great majority of even the shop craft employees are satisfied with the Pennsylvania Plan."[32]

The results in this case are all the more interesting because the two plans were in open competition. The men were vir-

[31] Bulletin of the Pennsylvania Railroad on the Plan of Employee Representation, p. 40.
[32] Ibid.

tually forced to choose between their national union and the Company's shop committees. The wages and regulations under which they chose to work were agreed upon between the management and employee representatives elected in the plant. The success of the Pennsylvania Railroad with its shop committes and the loyalty shown by its employees was a big factor in leading other roads to follow suit.

The real difficulty here faced by the unions was a breakdown within their own organization. The trade union is confronted, therefore, with the necessity of first converting employees to the superior advantages of the unions. If union employees cannot force recognition from the employer, it seems unwise to reject shop committees and so deprive themselves of any means of collective action. There is always the chance that continued pressure will result in union recognition. It is especially important that the union maintain a cordial and sympathetic relation with the non-union element. Otherwise it may happen, that when the need for greater strength and a broader organization is realized, the non-union men, through their shop committees, will ignore the trade union organization and develop one of their own.

In the second place, there is reason to think that in suppressing the shop committee the unions are blind to certain weaknesses in their own organizations and to the services that certain elements of the shop committee might render. From time to time critics of the trade union movement have pointed out where the unions were failing to function to their best advantage. If the shop committee could be of any assistance to the unions in these respects, it would seem unwise for the unions, especially at these critical times, to refuse to avail themselves of any advantages offered by the shop committee.

Among the various problems of the trade unions, three stand out as being especially adapted to solution through the use of the shop committee. They are: first, the relations between trade union officials and the rank and file; second, the ineffectiveness of organization by trades and crafts instead of by industries; third, the lack of a local shop organization for regular bargaining in matters of production and local interest.

It has been suggested by students of trade unionism that the growing centralization of power in the hands of trade union officials has been worked to put them out of touch with the needs and desires of the rank and file of trade unionists.[33] They have grown away from a knowledge of local shop practices, local conditions and local needs. In the words of one observer, trade union officials " are about as far away from the actual sentiments of their constituents, and I believe, from really leading them in a constructive manner as are the absentee landlords of business or the casual members of board of directors of large industrial establishments from the rank and file of their employees." [34] The workers have shown an increasing desire for a larger degree of self-government, for a more intimate participation in the negotiations in matters of labor policy and in their own shop. This is evidenced by signs of a lack of control by the leaders of the members of the union. One report has, in this connection, called attention to the unusual number of unauthorized strikes which have recently taken place.[35] It goes on to say:

The quickness with which the workers in many establishments have responded to the invitation of the employers to participate in a plan of representation embracing collective bargaining . . . is also significant of the desire of the workers towards some degree of self-government in their shops—a desire which the unions, under their present form of organization, fail to satisfy.[36]

On the part of employers, this same complaint finds expression in the growing antagonism to national agreements respecting wage scales, working schedules and regulations. There is an increasing demand on the part of employers that

---

[33] Cole, Self-Government in Industry.
[34] Quoted from a personal letter from the manager of industrial relations of one of the largest and most progressive corporations in the country.
[35] Report No. 18, Bureau of State Research of the New Jersey State Chamber of Commerce, p. 16.
[36] Report of the Bureau of State Research of the N. J. State Chamber of Commerce, p. 17.

such negotiations shall be carried on exclusively with their own employees or representatives elected from among their own employees.   The rapid extension of the shop committee following the breakdown of the shopmens' strike was largely due to the fact that the shop committee fitted in with the desire of the roads to avoid national agreements and to negotiate only with their own employees.

The outcome of the strike was a blow to the union's insistence upon national agreements.   Unless the unions are prepared in some way to meet this situation, the desire of their membership for a greater degree of self-government, coupled with the desire of employers to deal directly with their own men, may combine to work further injury to the national trade unions.

Furthermore, the inherent weakness of the organization of workmen by trades and crafts has been frequently pointed out.   The development of union organization along purely craft lines has been in total disregard of the evolution of modern industrial organization in which workers are concentrated in large shops, which have become even more natural units than the crafts themselves.   This has tended to impair the economic power of unions in those industries made up of a large number of unorganized crafts.   The waste and confusion occasioned by jurisdictional disputes, which arise directly from the overlapping of crafts in modern industry, are admitted by trade union leaders themselves.   One of their greatest problems is the prevention of this dissipation of power resulting from the endless number of conflicts among the various trades over their respective jurisdiction.   Another consequence has been the difficulty of maintaining the interests of the mass of the workers in the routine business of the organization.   All the important meetings of the union are conducted at various headquarters, more or less remote from the workshop where the constituency is located.   It is a frequent complaint of union officials that the meetings are poorly attended.   The members of the union " have in common with one another their membership in the same trade or industry,

but apart from general trade questions, they have few common preoccupations or problems.   They work as a rule for
various employers and the employees of a single firm are
scattered in a large number of district unions and branches." [37]

Probably the most serious defect of existing trade union
organization is the lack of any machinery or agents to handle
the many questions of purely plant or shop interest.   Outside
of the provision for conferences to negotiate the working
agreement and for the irregular visit of the business agent to
deal with grievances, the trade union fails to provide any
means whereby collective bargaining may take place as a
regular and normal process of industrial relations.

In part, the unions are not entirely responsible for this condition.   It is the logical outcome of that period of trade union
history when the unions were compelled by employers to
transact their business outside the shop and when workmen
were under the necessity of concealing their union membership from fear of discharge.   But more recently this condition has been due to an emphasis of the unions upon wages
and working rules to the neglect of the more local and intimate interests of workers, such as welfare, unemployment,
insurance, profit-sharing and production.[38]   The activity of
shop committees in these fields, increasingly important to the
workers, has been one of the chief objects of ridicule and
attack by the unions.

---

[37] Cole, Self-Government in Industry.   Mr. Cole has criticised severely the organization of the British labor movement upon the basis
of trades and crafts and his conclusions apply with equal force to the
movement in the United States.   He says: " The true basis of trade
unionism is in the workshops and the failure to recognize it is responsible for much of the weakness of trade unionism today.   The
workshop affords a natural unit which is direct stimulus to self-assertion and control by the rank and file.   Organization that is based upon
the workshop runs the best chance of being democratic and of conforming to the principle that authority should rest, to the greatest
possible extent, in the hands of the governed. . . .   More conscious
democracy is needed in the trade union movement and this, organization based on the workshop does at least help to provide."

[38] Prof. Barnett has pointed out that the trade unions are not well
qualified to exercise much influence on the sanitation, health conditions,
and other welfare features of the workshop, and have not paid much
attention to them.

As a consequence, participation of the workers in the performance of functions of increasing importance to them, has remained outside the scope of trade union activity. Quoting again from the report of the New Jersey State Chamber of Commerce: "In other words, the union organization under this arrangement has not broadened its functions and granted self-government to the workers in the shops to a degree sufficient to raise the interests of the workers in union affairs and to promote greater responsibility and contentment all along the line."

The failure of the trade union to evolve or to encourage machinery for joint enterprise in the workshop is largely responsible for many of the basic faults of the trade union movement. It has prevented the union from understanding the problems of production as such, and is responsible more than anything else for the lack of sympathy shown towards the specialized needs and emergencies of the employer. The inelasticity of trade union policy, its inability to adjust itself to changes necessitated by conditions of industry may be traced directly to the absence of an intimate contact with everyday industry. The utter helplessness of the national trade union when confronted with a business depression and its inability to make ready adjustments has been laid to two causes: (1) lack of a fundamental knowledge of business and (2) the absence of any responsibility for the welfare and success of the industry. The usual campaign of the typical national union for higher wages, shorter hours and better working conditions works well in a period of prosperity and rising prices, but fails in periods of deflation and falling prices. It has indeed been charged, that outside of these objects, the typical trade union has no other policy or purpose.

The opportunities which the shop committee affords for the adjustment of grievances and for the consideration of complaints involving discipline and promotion is one of its strongest elements. Each individual workman is vitally interested in the redress of his own grievances and can be counted upon to support any form of organization which offers this opportunity. Professor George E. Barnett has pointed out the importance of this consideration to the trade unions. The success of the railroad brotherhoods is accounted for in large measure by the provisions which they have made for protecting the interests of the worker in matters of discipline and promotion. Professor Barnett says:

[These provisions . . . operate to give every member of the brotherhoods a direct personal interest in the activities of his union. It is a fact of common observation in the study of trade unions that those unions are strongest, other things being equal, in which the work of the union affects the member solely as an individual.

The desire to raise wages or shorten hours is a mass desire and in experience has proved less strong than the desire to resist unjust discharge or discrimination. Where a piece rate, for example, must be the subject of constant bargaining, the desire of the worker to put behind himself the strength of the union is apparently more effective than the desire to cooperate in raising the standard rate.[39]

The failure of the majority of trade unions to provide permanent, local machinery for the adjustment of grievances as they arise in matters of discharge and promotion is a fundamental weakness of the movement.

Above all, this absence of any provision for normal association between employees and employer in the individual plant has prevented any progressive improvement in the spirit of the relations between the two. The attitude of suspicion and antagonism prevailing between the two classes is but a product of the emphasis placed by each upon their militant activities. All policies are subordinated to the upbuilding of economic strength. Even insurance policies, old age, unemployment insurance and benefit features of all kinds have for their primary purpose the maintenance of the power to strike on the one side and the power to resist on the other. The national trades unions and the employer associations may be likened to armed camps, industrial relations to a series of battles, and the psychology of each to the psychology of war.

But enough has been pointed out to suggest the possible ways in which the shop committee may be of service to the trade union movement. The modifications suggested by the

---

[39] Paper read before the thirty-fourth Annual Meeting of the American Economic Association, Pittsburgh, Pa.

granting of self-government to employees through their shop committees would tend to strengthen the relations between the leaders and the rank and file and bring about a much needed democracy in the whole trade union organization. The substitution of the shop for the trade or craft as a basis of union organization would increase their effectiveness in shop committee would require adjustments in trade union organization urgently demanded by the trend of events. The the industrial struggle and their capacity fcr efficient cooperation in constructive activity. Finally, the acquisition of the shop committee as a part of trade union organization would make possible a closer touch with the particular problems of the several industries, would bring within the scope of union activities the various welfare and service features of the modern corporation and would ultimately tend to overcome the war psychology and replace it by a spirit of cooperation based upon understanding.[40]

There is, in fact, much to be said in favor of a reversal by the trade unions of their present policy and a return to the attitude prevailing during the war period; when trade union leaders saw many possibilities for good in shop committees and viewed them as a good beginning for the unorganized and as a desirable asset to the union organization in the settlement of local grievances. Indeed, the abandonment of the policy of antagonism is much more imperative at the present time. The trade unions might as well realize that the shop

---

[40] The Report of the President's Second Industrial Conference dealt with this problem of the trade union: "The union has had its greatest success in dealing with basic working conditions, and with the general level of wages in organized and partially organized industries and crafts. . . . Local problems, however, fall naturally within the scope of shop committees. No organization covering the whole trade and unfamiliar with special local conditions and the questions that come up from day to day, is by itself in a position to deal with these questions adequately, or to enlist the cooperation of employer and employee in methods to improve production and to reduce strain. Except in trades in which the union itself has operated under a system of employee representation, as it does in shipbuilding and in the manufacture of clothing and in other trades, these internal factors are likely either to be neglected or to be dealt with in a way which does not make for satisfactory cooperation."

committee has too many worthy features to be either totally disregarded or ruthlessly set aside. The union would have nothing to lose by cooperation and it has much to gain; on the other hand persistent hostility may in the long run result in great injury both to the trade union and to the shop committee.

Realizing this, a far-sighted trade union leadership would set about devising the best means of coordinating the shop committee with the union organization and, if necessary making fundamental adjustments in the constitution of the trade union movement.[41] In order to maintain a sympathetic contact with shop committees, the trade unions could afford to admit them as locals, even though the national unions had no part in the bargaining and although membership was entirely honorary. The ultimate objective would be the adoption of the shop committee as a working part of trade union organization.

The advantages of the shop committee as a functioning unit of the national trade union have been pointed out by students of the two movements. First, it would " furnish an excellent instrumentality for applying and interpreting the terms of the labor agreement made with the union." [42] Second, it would " enlist the worker's interest in production to a much greater extent than at present." [43] Third, " the leaders will realize that decentralization and transfer of certain of

---

[41] Mr. Stoddard conceives this process of adjustment to be already taking place both in the unions and in employers' associations. " Both the labor union and the employers' union are in process of changing their functions and of adjusting themselves to the new forms of joint union based on the principles laid down in the previous chapters as the principles of the shop committee. It is now, therefore, seen to be the fact that the shop committee promotes unionism of the workers, just as it promotes unionization of the employers, but that it promotes this unionization for a fresh purpose and in a fresh way. Motive in human affairs is everything. The motive of the old labor union and of the old manufacturers' association was primarily defensive, hence militant, and hence to some extent destructive. The motive of the new union is constructive. It looks toward cooperation instead of competition, towards strife only as a last resort " (Stoddard, The Shop Committee, p. 99).
[42] Douglas, " The Shop Committee and the Trade Union," in American Journal of Economics.
[43] Ibid.

their functions to shop committees democratically elected on the floor of the plant, will help them to devote their attention to the broader problems of the labor movement affecting the entire trade or industry and assuming national or even international scope.[44]   Fourth, the shop committee would keep the union in close touch with the intimate details of industry, and enable it to adapt its policy to the particular needs and conditions in each individual plant.

Certainly the outlook for the trade union does not justify uncompromising hostility to the shop committee.   There are indeed a few signs that this is being realized.   A shop committee system exists in the Bethlehem Shipbuilding Corporation by an agreement between the Corporation and the Metal Trades Department of the American Federation of Labor. While the activities of the committees are limited mainly to welfare work and the presentation of grievances and while there are no joint committees, yet the arrangement is important as a first attempt to harmonize the central union organization with local self-government through shop committees. At the same time increasing pressure is being brought upon the trade unions to recognize the effectiveness of organization on an industrial basis.   The shop committee stands ready to assist the trade union in this transformation.   The most powerful and successful of the national unions, such as the United Mine Workers, the Railroad Brotherhoods, and the Clothing Unions, are organized on the basis of industries.

The Railroad Brotherhoods, in particular, seem to have adopted at least a tolerant, if not a sympathetic, attitude toward the joint shop committees recently set up by the Pennsylvania Railroad.   These committees were first organized among the men of the Engine and Train Service.   The local officials of the Brotherhoods actively cooperated in the establishment of these committees and now serve as representatives of the men.   The divisional joint committees are composed of the division superintendents and the local chairmen repre-

---

[44] Bulletin of Bureau of Economic Research of N. J. State Chamber of Commerce.

senting the engine and train service employees. The General
Superintendents and the General Chairmen of the Engine
and Trade Service unions meet monthly to hear appeals from
the divisional committees. Finally, the Joint Reviewing
Committee, the highest authority for settling disputes between the management and the men, is composed of two representatives of the management for each Region of the System and the nine General Chairmen of the Engine and Train
Service employees. This is the body which negotiates the
agreements regarding wages and working rules.

The local and general chairmen of the union are, of course,
employees of the Road. There has been no provision made
for the participation of the national officers of the Brotherhoods. Their attitude toward the arrangement is uncertain.
Either they have acquiesced in the action of the local officials
or they have been helpless to prevent it. The shop committee
system seems to have been built up within the national unions
and now appears to be functioning in harmony with them.
While the compromise has undoubtedly meant some sacrifice
in power on the part of the national officers, there still remains much for them to do. The economic strength of the
national unions remains unimpaired.

The outlines of a practical trade union policy towards the
shop committees seem fairly well defined. The establishment
of shop committees in fields impossible for the union to organize should be encouraged. With existing shop committee
systems, the unions should strive for a working arrangement
and above all for the sympathy both of the men and the employers. The employees should be urged to consider the advantages of a national organization, for protection, and for
the wider purposes of the labor movement such as standardized wages and labor legislation. The employer might well
be urged to consider the protection which a national organization gives him against the cut-rate competitor and the advantage of better cooperation in the whole industry. Finally, the
present national unions might well consider the installation of
the shop committee in all industries which they now control,

fully endowed with local authority, and fully coordinated with the national organization for the industry.

As matters stand at present, the shop committee and the trade union are more actively in competition than ever before. The shop committee has pushed its way into territory long controlled by the unions, who can be expected to exert every effort to regain their lost ground. On the other hand, the employers will endeavor to prevent it. The struggle has resolved itself into a competition for the loyalty of the employees. There will be ample opportunity for each system to demonstrate its superiority. In the long run, that system which appeals most strongly to the employees will win. The final verdict will be rendered by the great body of industrial workmen.

The shop committee may eventually prove to be an ally of the trade unions. The value of the shop committee as a stimulus to the desire of the workmen to organize has been either overlooked or underestimated. The unions have always urged that training in their organization is a necessary preparation for successful shop councils. But the rule works both ways. The experience and the habit of collective dealings gained through the shop committees may well be a preparation, may well stimulate the desire of the employees for a larger share in management, for the more powerful collective bargaining of the trade unions.[45]

---

[45] Mr. W. L. Stoddard, in discussing the relations between the shop committee and the trade unions, takes much the same position. He says: " Wholly outside the relationship established by shop committees between men and management in given plants, is the relationship between the shop committee and the general labor movement. We have seen that the establishment of a shop committee system in a factory does not in theory at least bring about union recognition, and that it does not, in theory once more, encourage unionism. But does it not in fact advance the tenets of unionism in general? Is not the shop committee a training school in industrial organization, and will not the workers thus taught the advantages and technique of organization, incline more and more to enter the wider field of labor organization as represented by the trade union? Is it a fair statement of the case to say that the shop committee is at best a temporary expedient designed to avoid the apparent recognition of the union, while in reality recognizing the essential principles of the trade union? " (Stoddard, The Shop Committee, p. 96). The only criticism

The shop committee sets forces at work whose ultimate consequences cannot be foreseen. Certainly, employees who have experienced representation through shop committees will never be satisfied with less. The chances are rather that they will desire more. It is inevitable that the workers, through their shop committees, will be led on, step by step, to an increasing participation in industry, to a fuller share in the responsibilities of production, and ultimately to some form of a national organization covering the whole industry. It is not likely that the shop committee will permanently deprive itself of a broader association. It will naturally extend itself over the industry. The trade union stands ready to profit by this inevitable development, unless it alienates itself from the beginning by an unreasoning and short-sighted policy of uncompromising hostility.

---

to be made of this view seems to be that the influence of the shop committee tends to undermine the trade union idea in favor of the industrial union. The shop committee is in reality in direct contrast to the essential principle of organization by trades and crafts.

INDEX

American Federation of Labor, resolution condemning shop committees, 31; executive committee on shop committee, 78; executive committee report at Montreal Convention, 83, 84; resolution on President's Second Industrial Conference, 84.

American Trade Union Movement, opposition to shop committee, 30, 31.

Appeal, right of representative to, 42.

Arbitration, provision for, 48.

Armour and Company, system of representation and committees, 36; composition of Plant Conference Board, 37; General Conference Board, 38; qualifications for voting, 40; qualifications for representatives, 41; provision for recall, 41; right of appeal for representatives, 42; meetings, 43; place and expense of meetings, 44; method of procedure, 46; voting, 47, 48; scope of committees, 50.

Authority, degree of, in shop committee, 51, 52.

Barnett, Geo. E., on strength of trade unions, 99.

Benefits of shop committees, 71, 72, 73–76.

Bethlehem Shipbuilding Corporation, shop committees joined with trade unions in, 102

Bethlehem Steel Company, wages and hours, 57; action on grievances by shop committees, 62.

Bridgeport Award, system of divisional committees, 36; general joint committees, 37; qualifications for representatives, 41; methods of voting, 47.

Bridgeport Brass Company, wage adjustments by shop committee,

57; matters considered by meetings, 66.

Business depressions, effect upon shop committees, 54, 55.

Cole, G. H. D., quoted on self-government in industry, 97.

Collective bargaining, definition of, 9.

Colorado Coal Commission, report of, 17.

Colorado Fuel and Iron Company, annual joint meeting of, 38; arbitration in plan of, 48, 49; wage reduction through committees, 59; attitude of union toward shop committees, 81.

Economic power, shop committee's lack of, 82, 89, 90.

Elections, qualifications for voting, 39, 40; time of, 41.

Elgin National Watch Company, shop committee action on profit-sharing, 57.

Employees, growth of shop committee among, 93, 94.

Employers, attitude of, toward shop committee, 30; interest in shop committee of, 74, 75.

Expense of shop committees, 44.

Exploitation, shop committee used as a means of, 91, 92.

Foster, W. Z., attitude toward shop committee, 80, 81.

General Joint Committee, composition of, 37.

Goodyear Tire and Rubber Company, plan of representation, 35.

Gompers, Samuel, on shop committee, 31, 79, 83; on Whitley Report, 77; on committees of Bethlehem Steel Company, 78.

Government agencies, success with shop committee, 26.